HUGO VON HOFMANNSTHAL

HUGO VON HOFMANNSTHAL

Poets and the Language of Life

Adrian Del Caro

LOUISIANA STATE UNIVERSITY PRESS

BATON ROUGE AND LONDON

Copyright © 1993 by Louisiana State University Press
All rights reserved
Manufactured in the United States of America

First printing

02 01 00 99 98 97 96 95 94 93   5 4 3 2 1

Designer: Amanda McDonald Key
Typeface: Palatino
Typesetter: Graphic Composition, Inc.
Printer and binder: Thomson-Shore, Inc.

Library of Congress Cataloging-in-Publication Data

Del Caro, Adrian, 1952–
    Hugo von Hofmannsthal: poets and the language of life / Adrian
Del Caro
        p.   cm.
    Includes bibliographical references and index.
    ISBN 0–8071–1786–2 (alk. paper)
    1. Hofmannsthal, Hugo von, 1874–1929—Criticism and
interpretation.   I. Title.
PT2617.O47Z7356   1993   92–22939
831'.912—dc20   CIP

The paper in this book meets the guidelines for permanence and durability of the Committee
on Production Guidelines for Book Longevity of the Council on Library Resources. ♾

für Anja Nicolina

CONTENTS

PREFACE

This *Hofmannsthal* is an introduction to the poetry, and treats on a detailed basis the poems published during the 1890s and those few published later. My writing here is not "for" scholars of German, but certainly not "against" my colleagues either. Those who take an interest in the *fin de siècle*, in the influence of Friedrich Nietzsche's seminal writings of the 1870s and 1880s, and those for whom poetry is a living concept will find in my treatment of Hugo von Hofmannsthal's poetic work a threshold to the language of life, as suggested in my subtitle.

It was not my goal to offer interpretations of Hofmannsthal's poems, and where this appears to be the case, the reader should consider that each text is approached within the context of major dimensions of the early Hofmannsthal poetic. I attempted to let the poems speak for themselves, and this required a good deal of translation, all of it my own. But for the same reason that I eschew "total interpretations," I have also avoided total translation. It is one thing to try to reenact a poem by capturing as much of its lyricality as possible, but quite another thing to penetrate beyond the poetic devices of a poem in order to awaken its soul. Companion volumes should be consulted by readers wishing to see "polished" translations of Hofmannsthal's poems (*e.g.*, Michael Hamburger's 1961 edition in the Bollingen Series), or a comprehensive treatment of Hofmannsthal's work beyond poetry and into drama (*e.g.*, Benjamin Bennett's 1988 *Hugo von Hofmannsthal*).

I wish to thank my colleague Donald G. Daviau, editor of *Modern Austrian Literature*, for encouraging my interest in Hofmannsthal and certain other Austrian writers during the last decade. I am also grateful to the College of Arts and Sciences of Louisiana State University for a Manship Fellowship enabling me to complete this book.

HUGO VON HOFMANNSTHAL

1 *LEBENSPHILOSOPHIE*

Basic to my understanding of *Lebensphilosophie*, or the philoso-phy of life, is presence of life, on the one hand, and the expres-sion of that presence on the other hand. However poignant or keen one's experience of life may become, there are intervals of inertia between realization and apprehension, between appre-hension and the sharing of presence through language. Lan-guage here means articulation. The practitioners of the philos-ophy of life are expressive individuals whose extraordinary capacity for presenting life, as manifestation, induces them to articulate that presence in language. The most skillful and re-vered articulators of presence are poets, but only insofar as the poet is indeed a presence and has sufficient presence to share—articulators per se are not of necessity poets.

The translation of presence into language is hindered by the intervals of inertia, and this inertia can be described as result-ing from a collision between dynamic and static, between liv-ing and dying. However, the collision between presence and articulation does not result in a complete standstill, but in a falling off or slowing of activity, like abatement. For this reason, however alive and vibrant with presence the vision of the poet was originally, translated into the poet's work it begins imme-diately to die. Language has a lethal effect on all things. Fried-rich Nietzsche wrote that "every word is a prejudice" ("jedes Wort ist ein Vorurteil"), but I maintain that every word is a death sentence (*jedes Wort ist ein Todesurteil*).[1] For at another point Nietzsche was writing about self-esteem and the interval between experience and articulation: "Our actual experiences are not in the least communicable. They could not express themselves if they wanted to. This is so because they lack

1. Friedrich Nietzsche, *Menschliches, Allzumenschliches*, in *Werke in drei Bän-den*, ed. Karl Schlechta (Munich, 1966), I, 903. The title of this quip is "Danger of Language for Intellectual Freedom." Further references to the works of Nietz-sche will be made parenthetically in text by volume and page number, desig-nated as *Werke* in footnotes, all with respect to the three-volume Hanser edition.

words. We are already well beyond anything for which we have words" (II, 1005). But presence, as experience, is real, is actual, and we *are not beyond presence*. Consequently, to have presence we must not articulate, must not try to find the word for it—then we will not be "beyond" presence by virtue of having killed it with a word.

Language as the means of articulation is always dying. We speak of "dead languages" as those no longer having the capacity to change, because they are not in active use, not linked to the vitality of flourishing generations. When scholars and artists attempt to reconstruct or revive the culture of the ancients through their dead languages (Greek, Sanskrit, Latin), these efforts are not merely nostalgic; the youthfulness—indeed, infancy—of language as mankind's historical awakening, places us in the presence of more exuberant, more living life. The modern poet who expresses immediacy of presence will generally have a primitive effect, despite sophistication in the work. Hölderlin, more so than any poet since the Enlightenment, dwelled in the vital presence of the ancients by working himself back to a state of being in which language still called upon being to manifest a presence, as opposed to strict modern usage, in which language, as the medium of objectivity and objectification, labors to conquer territories in its own name even as it has forgotten its own name—disavowed its name.

Nietzsche's early effort to stand in the presence of the phenomenon life in order to serve as life's spokesman resulted for him in a harvest of objective criticism. In the 1870s, *The Birth of Tragedy* had to be misunderstood, it had to be judged according to the merits of objective scholarship. In the intellectual climate of today, however, the work exerts a quickening, invigorating effect. Nietzsche himself wished that he had done some things differently—the late chapters extolling Wagnerian opera continue to be an embarrassment—but what romantic work has ever been complete, let alone perfect? By the mid-1880s, Nietzsche was better able to understand what he had attempted and achieved in *Tragedy*, for by this time he had become an experienced philosophical campaigner. He was now unabashedly claiming to be the spokesman for life, and his philosophical writing illustrated his conviction that "all philosophizing up to now had not been concerned at all with 'truth,' but instead with something else, let us say with health, future, growth, power, life" (II, 12).

In "Attempt at a Self-Criticism," appended to *The Birth of Tragedy* in 1886, Nietzsche explained that in the face of any absolute morality, such as Christianity's, life is "crushed beneath the weight of contempt and an eternal No, as unworthy of being desired, as unworthiness itself." Morality, he continued, exerts the force of "a will to deny life" that acts as a secret instinct of annihilation, a "principle of decline, diminution, and disparagement, the beginning of the end." In hindsight he argued that *Tragedy* was the result of his own instinct "as a spokesman instinct for life," and the purely aesthetic, artistic-metaphysical tone of the work was intended to oppose the antilife values of Christianity (I, 15). However selective this interpretation of *Tragedy* may be, still there is no denying that Nietzsche felt quite at home in his pagan surroundings, and was sincere in equating the heightened capacity for suffering and beauty with an amoral, artistic phenomenon that is best called the Dionysian.

In *Tragedy* Nietzsche was still sufficiently romantic, sufficiently devout as a disciple of art to attempt an articulation of presence through the medium of artistic metaphysics. As yet unaware that he was "well beyond" everything for which he had words, he used an orchestra of words to advance and sustain his argument. When I say "as yet unaware," it is not without misgivings. In the essay "On Truth and Lie in an Extra-Moral Sense" (1873), Nietzsche had already demonstrated penetrating insight into language and its disposition. However, at this early date he had not yet gone through the ordeal that began with the publication of *Tragedy* and continued until he had to break with Wagner and abandon his professorship at Basle. We can speak accurately of a philosophy of life in Nietzsche only when he himself recognized the limitations of his early romantic position and began his exhaustive critique of the foundations of nihilism. *The Birth of Tragedy* is one of Nietzsche's rare "texts" in the sense that contemporary theory uses the term to define its objects of derision. In this sense too it is a vulnerable text because all texts have profile, extension, character—they are easy targets. But the later writings beginning with *Human, All Too Human* pose a different challenge, because they uphold Nietzsche's faith in human ability to articulate life, to share presence, without petrifying into a structure that necessarily falls short of life, and falls into inertia.

Nietzsche's cautious avoidance of ever again erecting a metaphysical edifice resembling *Tragedy* helped him to formulate the points, the footholds he was to use for articulating the philosophy of life. These "points," as I wish to refer to them, are subsumed in the German *Anhaltspunkte, i.e.,* holding points or, roughly, criteria, but in Nietzsche's antiteleological thinking they cannot be construed as bases or foundation. When in revisiting *Tragedy* Nietzsche spoke of *opposing* the instinct of life-denial with his own instinct for serving as life's spokesman, he was suggesting the relationship he had established with the foundations of Western thought. Everywhere this foundation and its structures are in evidence, sometimes towering and seemingly unassailable, as for instance metaphysics, sometimes dazzling and alluring, as for instance idealism, sometimes righteous and absolute, as for instance morals—he defined his work as the activity of opposing these monoliths. For all their venerability and sheer size, the monoliths are not presence, but the crushing and obscuring of presence. Life does not flourish in the monoliths, but somewhere else—indeed, *anywhere* else.

In "Morality as Anti-Nature" from *Twilight of the Idols* Nietzsche offered one of his most sustained commentaries on the intrusive, life-eroding effects of morals. "I will formulate a principle. Every naturalism in morals, that means every *healthy* morality, is ruled by an instinct of life; some command of life is fulfilled with a specific canon of 'Shall' and 'Shall not', some obstacle and hostile element on the path of life is therewith cleared aside" (II, 967–68). Here the primacy of life dictates its own morality, designated as a "naturalism" insofar as the instincts cannot do otherwise but clear life's path of obstacles. In the following section of "Morality as Anti-Nature" a similar relationship is described, this time formulated not as life and morality but life and values: "When we speak of values, we are speaking under the inspiration, under the point of view of life: life itself compels us to posit values, life itself values through us *when* we posit values." Consistent with his view that there are no "right" or "wrong" values, and that life is a value-positing phenomenon, Nietzsche concludes that the morality of anti-nature also reflects the value-positing of life, but of *declining life*, not life that ascends in vitality (II, 968). The declining life is the retreating life, the retiring of presence.

Tragedy was an attempt to present life by posing the modern person with Nietzsche's metaphysical reenactment of that moment in history when music becomes word, when intoxication becomes insight, when tragedy is born. Nietzsche found the vital presence of the ancient Greeks in early tragedy; these Greeks were most alive—they had not yet been infected by the Socratic disease of "theoretical optimism." Erich Heller explained in one of his late essays how in Nietzsche's eyes the "vulgar" Socratic dialectic subjects opponents to ridicule, but "this plebian pursuit of dialectic and logic is the worst offense against the fullness of life, against its plenitudes of contradictions that nurture the sense of tragedy." And I have argued elsewhere that Nietzsche despised the Socratic dialectic because it is a tool in the hands of *castrating* neuters who would neutralize or slacken life's inherent tensions.[2] As insistent as he was even in this early work that suffering and life-affirmation were the grist of art, still young Nietzsche's point of departure was a thoroughly romantic one. Contrast this attitude with his mature understanding of aesthetics. In *Twilight* aesthetics is described as either classical or decadent, depending on whether life is ascending or declining: "Aesthetics is indissolubly bound to these biological prerequisites: there is a *decadence*-aesthetics, there is a *classical*-aesthetics—'beauty in itself' is a hallucination, like all idealism" (II, 936).

By describing life as that which posits value, Nietzsche is saying that life, because it is presence, has the capacity to posit. If life were not present, its positing would be nothing more than radical romantic idealism, perhaps à la Fichte's *Ich*. As legitimate presence, life has a tendency to value through living things, to share or spread its presence, but it is interesting to note that declining life also shares itself, in its own kind and according to its own waning means. In this way Nietzsche escapes the noose of morality, for he does not insist on a good life as opposed to a bad life, but instead formulates his preference or affinity for ascending life. Only the ascending life has surplus (abundance, enduring presence) and for this reason does not require defending. Declining life, inasmuch as it tends to recede and requires constant propping-up, demands of its host a posture of rigid defense. Darwinian mentality dictates precisely at this point that life is at the apex, *i.e.*, when life *defends life*, but I agree wholeheartedly with Nietzsche when he claims in *Thus Spoke Zarathustra*, "Spirit is life that itself cuts into life" (II, 361). Life is not presence when it curls up into a posture of survival, but on the contrary, life is presence when it demonstrates the life-instinct by not defending life, but instead by splurging itself. An analogy from romantic theory might prove useful. Friedrich Schlegel claimed that the supreme law of *Poesie* is that it tolerates no law above itself, and therefore remains sovereign.[3] The sovereignty of life, removed now from aesthetics to philosophy of life,

2. Erich Heller, "Nietzsche and the Inarticulate" in *Nietzsche: Literature and Values,* ed. Volker Dürr, Reinhold Grimm, and Kathy Harms (Madison, 1988), 6; Adrian Del Caro, "The Pseudoman in Nietzsche, or The Threat of the Neuter," *New German Critique,* L (1990), 154–56.

3. Friedrich Schlegel, *Athenäums-Fragmente,* in *Kritische Friedrich-Schlegel-Ausgabe,* ed. Ernst Behler (Munich, 1958–), II, 182.

recognizes no master even at the expense of seeing itself expire; without subjectivity (consciousness, ego) life is incapable of defending itself—it is incessantly aggressive.

Christianity bears much of the brunt of Nietzsche's criticism because in it and through it the "self" comes up short. The most altruistic of religions has been responsible for maligning self. I view the most expressive of Nietzsche's works, *Thus Spoke Zarathustra,* as a modern person's articulation of the challenge of achieving selfhood. In *Ecce Homo* the Western collective morality is referred to as "the unselving morality" ("die Entselbstungs-Moral") (II, 1158). Nietzsche worked with language to bring us closer to the phenomenon "life" with less abstraction, less idealism, so that he practiced a use of language in which there are coinages and puns not—the deconstructionist must forgive me—for the sake of play, but for the express purpose of not being toyed or *played with* as a pawn of language. Heller has made it abundantly clear that Nietzsche was aware of his inconsistencies, and aware of the deceptions of language *without* reducing life to mere play. What Nietzsche feared more than anything and what drove him on to articulate the "paradigm of incompatibility" resonating in the mutually exclusive formulations of overman and eternal recurrence was the fear of the inarticulate and "the menace of rendering illegitimate *any* articulation of life through language."[4] Irony as the fundamental thought of all romanticism, despite Nietzsche's designation of himself as the world-historical antiromantic, is abundantly evident in Nietzsche's writings. His bright, sensitive use of language is not a retreat from language's insufficiency, but a frontal assault via language into those areas of thought that we had always considered sacrosanct. Nietzsche's play is not "neutral," as many poststructuralists would have it; instead, it is extremely aggressive and partial, especially insofar as the Nietzschean notion of play takes on the most dangerous game, namely, humanity's relation to language itself.

Where I find puns and wordplay in Nietzsche's text I do not immediately relativize the argument, construing the cleverness of his usage as license to dazzle on my own, as some drunken imitator. When Nietzsche writes of the *Entselbstungs-Moral,* therefore, I regard the concept as no less salient to his philosophizing than the concepts *self* and *morals.* Nietzsche's play is not gratuitous, and his imitators routinely forget that one must have the means to splurge and play

4. Heller, "Nietzsche and the Inarticulate," 9, 11, 8, 4.

before one is able to get away with it. The prefix *ent-* is found in many German words to connote removal: *Entfernung* is based on the stem *fern*, meaning distant, while the suffix-*ung* forms a substantive. The verb *entfernen* is "to remove" by placing distance, by placing something away. *Selbstung* would be a noun connoting the process of coming into selfhood, of asserting self, while *Entselbstung* describes a condition of "unselving" or "deselving."

However, I do not mean to imply that Nietzsche's terms are readily found in the German language, either in educated usage or in the vernacular; it is precisely his focus on the self, in the face of Western grammar orientation that deflects from the self, that prompted his inventiveness. Continuing now with his thought: "This single morality that has been taught hitherto, this unselving morality, betrays a will to the end, it *denies* life in the most basic way" (II, 1158). The basis of Christianity is altruism, deflection from the self, and in the early meditation "On the Use and Disadvantage of History for Living," Nietzsche claimed that Christianity glorifies one's last moment, the *memento mori*, because it is the culmination of our allegedly inferior earthly life and the beginning of our eternal life (I, 259). In other words, the *memento mori* "redeems" us once and for all from the bonds and travails of selfhood, from the lure and call of selfhood, in order to dissolve us into selfless bliss.

Nietzsche is careful to point out that the unselving morality is the only one that has been taught, and subsequently learned, testifying to its success as a code and explaining its longevity. The eternal recurrence of the same is Nietzsche's pointed rejoinder to the *memento mori*, for with it he establishes the *memento vivere* forever. Viewed as a moral code in itself, or more accurately, as an antimorality, the eternal recurrence of the same challenges one to focus always on the moment of life presently at hand, for the same life in all details is supposed to recur eternally.

When Nietzsche spoke as the *active* nihilist, he wished not to disavow nihilism per se, which colors all modern thought, but only that passive nihilism that surrenders and despairs in the face of meaninglessness. If earlier the meaning of life had been tied to God, religion, science, or any other dominating ideal, the retreat of the ideal leaves a vacuum—nihilism. Life, however, does not cease in the face of the ideal's retreat, only thought, only hope, only desire ceases, in the most severe cases. With the death of God, in Nietzsche's deliberately dramatic scenario, life is therefore *released* from its enslavement to the ideal; it is both free to fend for itself and free to despair if life is not strong enough to prevail. Nietzsche wrote that "in order to liberate life one shall have to annihilate morality" (III, 887). Morality is the ideal's mightiest fortress, its "Edel sei der Mensch," its most clever and *seemingly* beneficent illusion. But while morality is the tool of abstract Man, it is the powerful and insidious usurper of *homo vivens*.

When Nietzsche discoursed on liberation and release, he had a specific, vital case in mind: his own. For this reason, the forewords he appended to his earlier works function in the same lively, interactive manner as his major works: They come to grips with experience, they subject immature experience and thought to the unrelenting scrutiny of life. So for example in the foreword to *Human* he discussed his feeling of emancipation from Wagnerian romanticism and his subsequent invention of more appropriate company, namely, the free spirits. In the terrifying interval between faith, friendship, idealism, and the search for one's own life, Nietzsche learned to respect the role of perspective. Perspectivism has to be recognized and accepted, especially in the realm of values and with respect to living: "You must learn to comprehend the *essential* injustice in every For and Against, injustice as inseparable from life, and life itself as *premised* [*bedingt*] on perspectivism and its injustice." This argument against absolute valuations, a very *honest* argument, attempts to give to life what is life's, even at the expense of abject disappointment. For Nietzsche goes on to explain that the greatest perceived injustice is wrought by "life in its smallest, narrowest, paltriest and most nascent" forms; life cannot do otherwise, even in its flimsiest manifestations, than to *assert itself* as the end of all development, to assert itself against everything else, including "the higher, the greater, the richer" (I, 443). In this sense, the expression "to be cheated by life" carries new meaning; life does not grant wishes, or provide opportunities, or give chances—instead, it is capable of undermining everyone and everything that stands in its way, for it is the primal force.

Nietzsche's most affirmative creation, Zarathustra, is faced with the challenge of unconditional affirmation before he can embrace the eternal recurrence of the same. His nausea, in part, is caused by the realization that even the lowliest, meanest creatures and circumstances recur eternally—neither Zarathustra nor anyone else exercises choice in the matter. Perspectivism, then, cannot be adopted piecemeal. Since justice or what we might call the mortal's sense of propriety (his measure, his *proprium*) is not woven into the fiber of life, it is only natural that this sense of justice should be offended by the presence of low life, "mere" life chipping away at lives and cultures that have already risen to beauty and power. And yet, on what extramoral basis can one condemn this phenomenon? By which standards or measures does inexorable life, amoral, blind, and greedy, deserve condemnation? And what means, besides mere disparagement and cursing, would suffice to condemn? To what effect? Nietzsche wrote that there is no such thing as free will, only strong will and weak will (II, 585). The usefulness of "free will" he explained as a theological holdover; as long as man can choose, he can err, and therefore be punished and condemned (II, 997). The tolerance that Nietzsche demands as a result of recognizing perspectivism, however, is not to be confused with some playful neutrality, or with the mistaken assumption that Nietzsche was a drunken mystic who pronounced that all things were equally valid. Given Nietzsche's omnipresent observation that what is lacking in the human situation is presence of life, it is pointless to argue that he is a nihilist of the old or "passive" guard.

Life itself is value, life itself values through all living things—that is Nietzsche's response to run-of-the-mill nihilists. It is true, there is no good life versus bad or evil life, but there is life in varying degrees of intensity, strength, and presence, subjected to different interpretations and perspectives depending on its own needs. The basic character of life, ultimately, is a positive force, insofar as Nietzsche has opted unequivocally for life: "In all correlations of Yes and No, of preference and rejection, love and hate, only a perspective, an interest of certain types of life expresses itself: in itself, everything that is speaks with a Yes" (III, 788). By this reasoning, the perspective of life-types will display variations, perhaps even variations as multifarious as the different types of life themselves, but this does not change the fact that before "filtering" through the type, life is affirming.

Nietzsche's philosophical position on metaphysics in general, and on truth in particular, has been the most lucrative in terms of influence on twentieth-century thought. Heidegger for example has contributed to a reception of Nietzsche as the so-called last metaphysician, and taking its cue from Heidegger, poststructuralism continues to profit from the notion that Nietzsche's thought needs to be taken a step further, that in itself it is not sufficiently liberated from metaphysics. In the matter of the philosophy of life, it is my view that commentators have not given Nietzsche credit by exploring or unpacking the implications of his denial of metaphysics, but instead they place

Nietzsche under arrest, freezing him at various stages of his argument in order to offer, and to be able to offer, their own interesting "improvements" on his thought.

In *The Gay Science* Nietzsche cautioned that the "will to truth" can be more than a harmless "Don Quixotery," that it can actually be "a destructive principle hostile to life." Truth as a function of science, a pursuit of science, is based on a Platonic-Christian bias that there is a God, that God is the truth. So deeply rooted is this idealism, moreover, that even the antimetaphysical strategies of Nietzsche himself and his kind "steal their fire" from the metaphysical conflagration ignited by Christianity, insofar as even the free spirits, those endeavoring to liberate themselves from idealism, from metaphysics, are caught up in extracting the "truth" (II, 208). That point at which morality and science touch again on the question of life is achieved when, in recognizing the God-ideal and its powerful gravitational force as an error, nothing more than a monumental lie, we attempt to find ourselves in the absence of prescribed order.

Nietzsche ironizes the fact that throughout history philosophers have struggled with the greatest might not to be deceived—it is part of their "bourgeois" upbringing in the world of respectable, accountable, consensus values—and they of all persons do not wish to be faulted with "bad character." It would be bohemian for a philosopher to be faulted with "bad character," and Nietzsche thinks the philosophers strove too hard for one thing above all others: respectability. However, according to Nietzsche "it is no more than a moral prejudice that truth is worth more than appearance; it is in fact the most poorly proved assumption in the world." He claimed there would be no life if not for perspective estimations and appearances—there is no compelling need for the opposing of "true" with the judgment "false." Is it not sufficient, he asked, "to assume stages of appearance, as if with lighter and darker shades and overall tones of appearance?" (II, 600). Again, it is fundamental to Nietzsche's philosophizing for life that the subject/predicate, good/bad dichotomies are not essential. Consequently, it might do the species a certain amount of "good" if we simply accepted as a fiction the world "that concerns us." My reading of this argument stresses "what concerns us." Nietzsche had sufficient faith in humankind to trust that we have reached a point in our evolution where we no longer pin our collective integrity to whether we are in hot pursuit of "reality" or "fiction." In other words, whatever it is that we pursue as a species, and not merely as tribes within the species, this pursuit is a vital one, linked inextricably to the value-positing agency of life.

For Nietzsche understood better than most that even though we are disdainful of deceptions, we nonetheless are capable of deceiving ourselves and others. The moral code of Western man preaches against making judgments, yet we are constantly at work to refine and strengthen our judgments even while we try to distance ourselves from our work by remaining "objective." It is as if there were a judging, valuating mechanism in each of us, impossible to silence, impossible to switch off, a force that represents more than mere survival and therefore engages in activity that goes beyond the pale of mere survival. And for this reason Nietzsche referred to Darwinian "struggle for *existence*" as an assertion without sufficient proof. "It occurs, but as an exception; the overall aspect of life is *not* distress, not starvation, but wealth, abundance, even absurd squandering— where the struggle occurs, it is for *power*" (II, 998–99). In Nietzsche's orientation the need for a classical world view is apparent; with surplus and squandering as the rule, what is needed is form, articulation, and balance. We practice restraint in our capacity as articulating beings, and presence that is not articulated through the channeling of our surplus merely goes unnoticed, or perhaps it goes awry.

Declining life according to Nietzsche finds its voice in the dogma of Christianity, in Schopenhauer's philosophy of denial, and generally in idealism, while superabundant life poses for us the concept of highest affirmation and unconditional Yes-saying (II, 1109). Here Nietzsche's language has a dissuasive effect on some, who justifiably inquire into the meaning of "highest affirmation" and "unconditional Yes-saying." Though Nietzsche was the affirmative philosopher of life, the spokesman *for* life and life's articulator, rather than life's ongoing editor-commentator, still we have to admit that he is history's most *anti* thinker. This results, largely, as a consequence of language, and more specifically, that great interval between the comprehension of presence and its articulation that must always be bridged by language.

Nietzsche is more persuasive and appealing to poststructuralists, therefore, when he exercises the *anti* in deconstructing the edifice of Western epistemology. The greatest affirmative work, on the other hand, is *Thus Spoke Zarathustra,* couched in a language of affirmation that must draw heavily on symbolism and rhetorical intensity. Or as a case in point, consider the *Dionysus Dithyrambs* written as Nietzsche's major lyrical work, and these nine curious poems that owe their existence to the Zarathustra nexus. In "Fame and Eternity" the vitalistic link between necessity and affirmation emerges as a deeply personal, hymnic confession:

> Badge of necessity!
> Highest star of being!
> —that no wish attains,
> —that no denial besmirches,
> eternal Yes of being,
> eternally I am your Yes:
> *for I love you, o eternity!——*
>   (II, 1263)

The refrain from Zarathustra's roundelay serves as a vow spoken by Nietzsche in his symbolic marriage to eternity, and it is deliberately dramatic because, gifted as he was in his use of language, Nietzsche had no other means to articulate this solemn but at the same time affirmative act of union.

In his notes Nietzsche discussed the will to power as a "primitive form of affects" of which all other affects are only variations. This reminds us of the published context in which the same idea was expressed, namely *Beyond* No. 36, where the "intelligible character" of the world is reduced to the will to power. Continuing from his notes, he claimed that it is enlightening to view the individual life in pursuit not of happiness but of power. "It strives for power, for *more* in power." Consequently, pleasure according to Nietzsche "is only a symptom of the feeling of power achieved, a consciousness of difference" (III, 750). This brings to mind Schopenhauer's definition of pleasure from *The World as Will and Representation;* since willing and acting are, in reality, one operation, and every act of the will is also a manifest act of the body, impressions upon the body are likewise impressions upon the will. An impression counter to the will is called pain, while an impression in accord with the will is called pleasure.[5] Of course, Schopenhauer's ultimate end is to deny life-will, not to remove obstacles to its unfolding, as in the case of Nietzsche.

The superabundance of life and the individual's capacity to exercise restraint and volition result, in the best instances, in particularly strong, affirmative beings. Nietzsche considered Goethe to be of this mold; he also attributed this quality to Napoleon. From the notes:

5. Arthur Schopenhauer, *Die Welt als Wille und Vorstellung,* in *Werke in zwei Bänden,* ed. Werner Brede (Munich, 1977), I, 151.

"*Napoleon* . . . 'Totality' as health and highest activity; the straight line, the rediscovery of great style in action, the most powerful instinct, that of life itself, the lust to rule affirmed" (III, 633). This "lust to rule" is German *Herrschsucht,* derived from *herrschen,* to rule, and *sucht,* the substantive used to connote greed, lust, and even addiction. A person who is *herrschsüchtig* is therefore tyrannical (bent on ruling, on dominating). The expression "lust to rule" is no prettier, by our Judeo-Christian standards, than the expression "tyrannical." Nietzsche makes this the substance of his argument in "The Three Evils" in *Zarathustra. Herrschsucht* is cast in a positive light by Nietzsche, so he changes the expression to "the gift-giving virtue" in order to do justice to what ruling actually is as an expression of abundant life. It is already clear from the context of *Zarathustra* that Nietzsche is not talking about dictators and power-hungry demagogues: "The lust to rule: but who would call it *lust* when what is high longs downward for power! Verily, there is nothing rotten or greedy in such longing and climbing down!" (II, 437). Napoleon was a type whose fullness of life, whose fullness and directness of instinct, and whose strength to affirm his circumstances and destiny, shared himself by "coming down" among the peoples to shape events. This "coming down" is a necessity of power in the human realm; it is the articulation of presence expressing itself through rule.

The "coming down" of *Herrschsucht* offers an interesting glimpse into Nietzsche's perspectivism. He considered himself the philosopher of the heights because it is in high places that the surroundings are least hospitable and man is most likely to lose his way. Zarathustra is the prophet who comes down from his heights and solitude, only to discover that his particular virtue of giving is impossible for the community to receive. When Zarathustra retreats to his heights, the so-called higher men tentatively make their way to his home in the mountains, but ultimately they surrender to old ways and Zarathustra is without human company again. Community is not Nietzsche's strong suit—he was much more skillful in diagnosing the ills and dispositions of communities than he was in contributing to the establishment of community. The lust to rule "longs downward" for power because Nietzsche is prepared only to admit that community exists, and he will not go so far as to grant that community is deserving of any gift other than, or greater than, rule. And ultimately this Nietzschean perspective, with its cynical view of community and its seeming disavowal of communal values, is what contributes so richly to Nietzsche's illumination of *individual presence* through the denial of communal values—the Nietzschean individual arrives at self-hood by placing himself in opposition to the values of community. This view of course is totally consistent with Nietzsche's dictum that "the *goal of humanity* can not lie in its end, but instead only *in its highest exemplars*" (I, 270).

Napoleon was not a poet, but given Nietzsche's reasoning, had he been a poet his "gift-giving virtue" would have resulted in the work of art, and in the artist as the primary work of art. *Such a combination of life-abundance and affirmation had to result in an exemplary being.* But modern readers are inclined to view the juxtaposition of Napoleon, the ruler, and Goethe, the artist, as a fatuous one. This erroneous inclination, however, is based on our culture's denigration of the ruler, as well as its neutralizing of art. Nietzsche was adamantly critical of modernity's facile use of the term *l'art pour l'art*. Insofar as *l'art pour l'art* refers to the excising of morals from art, Nietzsche would be totally in favor, but it does not follow that if morals are banned from art, then so is any purpose or meaning. All art, according to Nietzsche, praises, glorifies, and selects, thereby strengthening some valuations and weakening others. This circumstance is not incidental, moreover, because the artist's deepest instinct is not directed toward art but to the meaning of art, *to life,* and to the *desirability of life:* "Art is the great stimulus to life: how could one regard it as without purpose, without goal, as *l'art pour l'art*?" (II, 1004).

It is easy to lose sight of why Nietzsche admired Napoleon, and Goethe, if the two are thought of merely as abstractions: Napoleon the Ruler, Goethe the Poet. The activity of each was secondary to the source of the expression—both were consummate practitioners of life, both were monumental in their embrace of life. If we wish to claim that both were gifted with genius, then let us also conclude that both heard and understood the language of life. Nietzsche's entire philosophizing can be viewed as the attempt to alert man to his potential, and to identify obstacles in the way of realizing potential. The greater part of this challenge lies in identifying obstacles, since Nietzsche was not disposed to remove them for us. If we remain unaware of obstacles, they do not function as levers to self-overcoming, and our ignorance of the obstacles presents us with a tranquil, vegetative view of life that encourages atrophy.

But Nietzsche's insistence that the articulating of life requires us to traverse a course of obstacles, in order to have something worthy of articulating in the first place, can easily be condemned as a romantic-quixotic quest. The danger of having to use poetic language to express the philosophy of life is that traditionally separated spheres, poetry and philosophy, vie with one another for attention. In Nietzsche, this circumstance contributes to his greatness and his weakness, and it also contributes to an almost rampant phenomenon in which thinkers, scholars, and artists trouble themselves with Nietzsche only to the point where they are capable of creating their own, better and more clever language. In so doing, they claim to honor Nietzsche by fulfilling his dictum that the pupil must overcome the master, but I see in this very little overcoming. Nietzsche's house is not hospitable to the frenzied and impatient, and scholarship today holds a very low opinion of mastery if so many so glibly overcome Nietzsche.

However Nietzsche may have stood in relation to life and its language, he generally fosters in his readers a greater love for both language and life. If Nietzsche was a poet, then surely he was the least naïve of poets. Naïveté and poetry go hand in hand—this is why poets are ashamed of themselves when they read their poetry, or why they ought to be ashamed. But this also is the virtue of poetry, that life has taken the poet by the hand, has led him astray, seduced and instructed him. The poets have always been embarking and returning, recounting their tales to any who will listen. Since the poets, unlike the philosophers, do not claim to instruct, and do not claim to practice correct thinking, we can turn to them in order to discover where life is capable of leading us.

Unlike Nietzsche's Zarathustra, the poets of this study do not tire of embarking and returning. The effective difference is that between poetry and philosophy. I think it is ironic, but at the same time quite understandable, that the poet Hölderlin, who became insane by the time he was in his mid-thirties, has captured the imaginations of our century's greatest philosophical minds—perhaps others consider it ironic that our century's philosophers have imagination, but that circumstance is entirely consistent with Nietzsche's view of the philosopher. Similarly ironic is how Nietzsche himself struggled to liberate himself from poetry in order to emerge as a philosopher; the "bourgeois" affliction of respectability among philosophers seems also to have haunted him. Many early Nietzsche commentators hailed him as a poet but refused to grant him philosophical respect.

If the language of life is ultimately not philosophical in the traditional sense of philosophical, that is, cognitive and rational, then perhaps it is because the phenomenon life, like the vast unconscious that speaks to us in dreams, presents itself in symbols rather than proofs, in lyric rather than rhetoric. It was the poet in Nietzsche that forced him to assert that life was the legitimate concern of philosophers, life as a biological phenomenon. But as he himself displayed the characteristics of a Janus complex, viewing life as a philosopher from one side and as a poet from the other, it is perhaps best if we turn to the poets who were themselves so full of life that their articulation is pure and close to the source. Heidegger suggested that the "purest speaking" of language is found in the poem.[6]

The embarking and homecoming poets know all there is to know about presence. Whatever can be known about presence, about life manifesting itself in the individual and coming to terms through speech, is known by poets. But it is also possible that nothing can be known about presence in the cognitive sense of knowing, and that "knowing" is a useless term. I say that the embarking and homecoming poets, borrowing terminology from Hölderlin and Nietzsche, know all there is to know about presence because they are the experts, they are the experienced ones whose frame of reference touches the *community* in which their poems are spoken, and the *source*, which is the destination of the sojourning poet and the scene of his trial, his vigil, his living while he is away from the community.[7] Unless the poet is himself a bridge between always-threatening isolation, a wilderness in which there is no speech, and community, where speech is both refined and simplified *in order to speak to mortals*—unless the poem draws into its circle of listeners source and community, there is no such thing as "pure speaking" of language.

Nietzsche appeals mightily to contemporary theorists in a variety of disciplines because his philosophizing is a useful tool for attacking "centrisms." And I would be the last person to argue against the basically healthy premise that institutions and the modes of discourse they engender require some taking down and taking apart from time to time—where Nietzsche encourages critical activity, and not merely critical thought, he is justifiably the hero of diverse groups. What is often overlooked, however, is that for all his critical acumen, Nietzsche was not content to serve as a critic. The point of departure for Nietzsche's critique of language is the same launching point from which most of his philosophizing, early and late, sets out—namely, vitalism. Nietzsche is the philosopher of life because he constantly,

6. Martin Heidegger, *Poetry, Language and Thought,* trans. Albert Hofstadter (New York, 1971), 72.

7. See Adrian Del Caro, *Hölderlin: The Poetics of Being* (Detroit, 1991), 99–117.

relentlessly held life and one's ability to live as the standard against which all else must be measured.

In *On the Use and Disadvantage of History for Living* Nietzsche described the main failing of the modern individual as a condition of lying at odds with oneself. The modern person, he claimed, carries within himself "an amazing collection of undigested knowledge-stones."[8] The undigested stones have the effect not only of rendering us all ponderous, but also of making a telltale noise that betrays "the remarkable antithesis of an interior without corresponding exterior, and an exterior without corresponding interior, an antithesis that the ancient peoples did not reveal." Knowledge simply absorbed without a corresponding hunger and *need* ceases to work as a formative principle contributing to one's total presence; instead, it accumulates uselessly within and moderns pride themselves on possessing a distinctive "innerness" (*eigentümliche "Innerlichkeit"*). The modern person then is accustomed to saying that content is not lacking, only form, but Nietzsche is quite clearly of a different opinion: "In all living things this is a thoroughly improper antithesis. Our modern education [*Bildung*] lacks vitality precisely because it cannot comprehend itself without this antithesis, that is, it is not real education at all, but a kind of knowing about education. It does not get beyond the concept of education, the feeling of education, and no educational resolution comes of it" (I, 232). Admittedly Nietzsche is asking for a lot when he demands that modern education contribute to a resolve as opposed to mass-producing future schleppers of stones.[9] The context here is a lack of vitality in education, and hindering vitality is the modern mindset or fixed idea that, as individuals, we are fine on the inside (supposedly ripe with content) but simply lack the means (time, ability, motivation?) to translate the interior qualities into a holistic presence. The antithesis is modern according to Nietzsche, not known to the ancients, and certainly we are dealing here with more than the romantic longing for unity with nature. Nietzsche engages the issue of modern education and claims, justifiably, that modern education does not contribute to living per se but only to conceptualizing and emoting about life.

8. Nietzsche is alluding to the fairy tale "Der Wolf und die sieben jungen Geißlein" in Grimms' *Kinder und Hausmärchen*.

9. I borrow from the verb *schlepp* because in its Yiddish form, familiar to most English speakers, it accurately describes what the stone-bearers do. Nietzsche's exact words are "Der moderne Mensch schleppt zuletzt eine ungeheure Menge von unverdaulichen Wissenssteinen" (I, 232).

In the same philosophical essay Nietzsche elaborated on his claim: "Within the realm of historical education philosophy is without rights if it wants to be more than an inwardly restrained knowing without effecting." Philosophy is tolerated because as moderns our trepidation for engaging life prohibits us from banning philosophy outright: "Yes, we think, write, print, speak and teach philosophically—everything is permitted to this extent; but it is different with respect to our actions, in so-called life: here only one thing is permitted and everything else is simply impossible" (I, 240). The ironic "in so-called life" should present a clear rationale for Nietzsche's emergence as the philosopher of life. Where everything really counts, in life as opposed to within the classroom, within academe, philosophy has no authority, has no rights.

In his blistering attack on the eunuchs of objectivity, Nietzsche pointed out how knowledge as bulk and ballast has learned to speak a language of its own, divorced from the phenomenon life. Primary in the semantics of nonlife is the concept of objectivity, for this notion legitimizes an otherwise vacuous existence. Nietzsche remarks that even while so much is being said of the "free personality," one really does not see any personalities at all. "The individual has retreated to the inside: on the outside this is no longer noticed." [10] If Nietzsche is to be taken seriously on this issue of the lapsing of identity, and the attending disadvantages accruing to life in the facile observance of the inside/outside antithesis, then clarification must be given about what life is becoming. Is Nietzsche holding the modern person to an impossible standard? Is his plea for truthfulness (*Wahrhaftigkeit*) and other qualities of strong character as they are paraded in theory in his essay merely a cry in the wilderness?

Recent developments in mass communication, especially in the medium of television, deserve close attention in the spirit of Nietzsche's critique of moderns. *Simulation* has become a media buzzword and, apparently, a legitimate reporting device. Where information has to be transmitted, it has become convenient to simulate incidents when actual footage of events is not available. Television programming also has its share of simulation-type programs designed to show the public how a crime might have looked as it was being perpetrated. Another category of simulation connected with television is in adver-

10. For a detailed treatment of Nietzsche on objectivity and the neuter, see Del Caro, "The Pseudoman in Nietzsche."

tising; those who wish to lose ugly excess pounds watch a simulated laboratory team simulating the discovery of a miracle formula. Simulation is obviously an invaluable tool for training people to perform difficult tasks, as in flight simulation. We have had reporting and acting for centuries, but new technology and new attitudes are now opening the door to simulation. Simulation is by no means limited to the recent technological applications mentioned above; indeed, it was Nietzsche's view that humans who lose the strength to prioritize living become doomed to simulate life—and it doesn't even show on the outside.

Simulation is modern both by virtue of the novelty of simulating techniques and technology, and by virtue of the loss of self that encourages simulation and allows it to creep into our lives. The tolerance for simulation is at issue here, as well as its need, given our supply-and-demand cultural programming. Unlike acting, which is generally understood to be acting, simulation purports to be nearly as good as the real thing; it is utilitarian in its conception, providing a service in lieu of having the genuine event at hand. A man who goes through life pretending to be a physician, while in reality he flunked out of medical school in the first year, is not simulating a physician's life—he is acting the part and cleverly manipulating the expectations of those who require the services of a physician. When the acting physician is discovered, moreover, society does not reward him with its approbation, generally in spite of any success he may have had as a healer, because he tried to deceive. However, the simulating physicians of the television fat-pill commercial are not "acting" in the traditional sense of acting, but merely simulating events that appeal to the viewers who are desperate to shed pounds. If this is perceived to be a small difference, or no difference at all in the minds of some people, what, then, accounts for the general acceptance of simulation when it is practiced on millions by the news media?

When we accept simulation, we are forfeiting a great deal more than the effort or ability required to make fine distinctions. The acceptance of simulation encourages the life-negating dualism engendered by the inside/outside antithesis, for an individual may always reason that somewhere deep inside, supposedly where it counts, a genuine and unadulterated person resides. This has the effect of relieving the individual of responsibility in the outer world of social interaction where, after all, things don't matter so much (Nietzsche's "so-called life"). One is tempted to retreat inward, not for the purpose of reflection designed to influence and inform the actions of a strengthened character, but simply for purposes of remaining concealed, cast away within oneself.

Nietzsche was sensitive to the shaping cultural factors of his day; his interest in a person's upbringing was anything but casual, anything but academic. If education in his century did not meet the challenge of engaging life head on, he at least struggled to emerge as the spokesman for life and the philosopher of life, attempting to illuminate the phenomenon that had vexed and eluded earlier philosophers. And what of education today? Is it sufficient to state that educators are involved in the activity of preparing people for life? Should educators retreat to the safer terrain of perhaps educating people for their society? If the latter position is adopted, education will result at best in persons who are taught to function in society, and even this is frequently beyond the reach of education.

It is not education that is at fault in any approach to the problem of educating humans. But that education remains on the outside, that internalized knowledge does not automatically result in a cogent presence free of the fraudulent antithesis of inside/outside—that is the realization that educators are coming to. If parents and students are prepared to pay the going rate, and to go through the proper motions, young people can enjoy a simulated education that prepares them sufficiently for a simulated life.

One can and I hope will object, pointing out that *my* education and *my* life cannot be simulated. After all, these are my experiences, my turmoils, triumphs, *my* results for better or worse—simulation cannot apply to *me* because I am real and simulations are not. Any person with a drop of blood in his veins would rise up and defend his life as life, and that person would of course be right. The philosopher, the critic, the theorist who stands before even the most meager specimen of human being and has the gall to proclaim, You are not alive! deserves to be laughed out of town. The important concern always seems to be *what do we mean by life?* No matter how we turn it around, it always comes back to life, the question itself comes to life.

And once again I find myself making room for the poet where the philosopher dares no longer speak. What is Nietzsche suggesting when he criticizes the results of education, and what does it mean when he pillories the institution of philosophy for degenerating into academics, into mere scholarship and criticism? Let us consider well that Nietzsche himself has been appropriated by the academic establishment. Despite his best efforts to remain *vogelfrei,* when he speaks even as the "philosopher of life" he cannot ordain what life is and should be.[11] If the philosopher has failed historically, as Nietzsche maintained, and if Nietzsche himself has fallen prey to scholars and their probing, unrelenting critical stare, still we do not have to let go of the standard that Nietzsche strove to keep. On the subject of life the proper medium is poetry, for poetry is not haunted by the antithesis of inside/outside. Instruction in living is needed, so says the philosopher, but it is the poet who gives instruction in living.

Ultimately the question of life's meaning is unfair. Poets do not choose to instruct—the best poets are not pedantic, didactic, prescriptive, dogmatic. For this reason, and perhaps *best* for this reason, namely, that the poets are naïve and disavow the role of teacher, they are heard when the philosophers are not heard.

11. This term means literally "free as a bird," but it was used during the feudal age to describe one who becomes an outlaw and is therefore declared *vogelfrei, i.e.,* outcast, beyond the protection of the law and not to be sheltered by anyone.

2 WORDS

Hugo von Hofmannsthal (1874–1929) published most of his poetry before 1900. The poems began to appear in 1890 under the pseudonym Loris Melikow, shortened to "Loris" and used until 1892 for the poetry, 1897 for some of the prose that appeared in Austrian and German periodicals. Gifted far beyond his years both in the ability to penetrate great writing (Goethe, d'Annunzio, Nietzsche) and to demonstrate insight as a literary critic and poet, Hofmannsthal's respect for language guarded him from trivial articulation.

Werner Metzler has pointed out that "genuine love poems" are almost completely lacking in the published poems of Hofmannsthal, and that he "strived to keep everything of a purely private nature far away from his writings."[1] The importance of this fact should be considered in light of Hofmannsthal's youth; despite the force of love in adolescence, and despite the thrill of seeing oneself initiated into the ranks of adulthood, this poet was capable of refining his expression and limiting the intrusion of the personally confessional—an amazing accomplishment for any poet, all the more amazing for a youth. But Hofmannsthal was not a cold, unfeeling person impervious to emotionalism. In fact, his sensitivity and empathy mark him as a natural poet, while his critical ability enabled him to extract from experience the essence that translates into poetry.

In his second published poem, "Question" ("Frage"), Hofmannsthal already indicated a major concern of his work; the relationship between art and life, between word and deed. The question is posed to a familiar other who is incapable of sensing the poet's difficulty; though he smiles to disguise his torture and deceit, the poet is exploring the other, trying to ascertain that person's feelings. The second strophe explains the basis of the poet's troubled relationship:

1. Werner Metzler, *Ursprung und Krise von Hofmannsthals Mystik* (Munich, 1956), 60.

Don't you long for a breath of life,
For hot arms to carry you away,
Beyond this swamp of dreary, barren days
Hemmed in by light too pale, too weak?[2]

The poet is beginning to realize that he has deceived himself, or has let himself be deceived, by the appearance of substance. What he had perceived in the other's gaze, namely, depth, a secret longing, and a passage from the eyes to the soul that would suggest authenticity and wholeness of being, turns out to be otherwise.

The wishes that slumbered there,
Like quiet roses in the flood, darkly,
Are like your small talk, soulless . . . words, words?
(*KA*, I, 8)

The other's gaze does not penetrate to the soul; it is therefore without soul, and the moist eyes, though beautiful in their dark background, are helpless to break out of their barren limitation—they do not long for the "breath of life." The small talk (*Plaudern*) is equated with the other's "slumbering dreams"; they will never awaken, apparently, since they too are without soul and amount to mere words.

"Question" published in 1890 demonstrates that Hofmannsthal was not mesmerized by beauty, and that he understood how beauty stands in competition with life for the poet's attention. Hofmannsthal chose the path of life as opposed to beauty, or at least he chose to elevate life while permitting beauty to unfold in the medium of living. What Meyer-Wendt has written concerning the early prose I embrace as well for the poetry, that "the call for life, for real experience is the most discernible criterion." Michael Hamburger speaks of Hofmannsthal's "passing addiction to Nietzsche's vitalism . . . then again a concern with the forms of social life, style in life rather than in art, pointing to Hofmannsthal's later solution of the antimony between art and life."[3] Hamburger's dismissal of Hofmannsthal's encounter with Nietzschean philosophy, and his dismissal of vitalism as "Nietzsche's vitalism," is in error.

---

2. Hugo von Hofmannsthal, *Gedichte 1*, in *Sämtliche Werke. Kritische Ausgabe*, ed. Eugene Weber (Frankfurt, 1984), I, 8. Further reference to this edition will be given parenthetically in the text as *KA* followed by volume and page number.

3. H. Jürgen Meyer-Wendt, *Der frühe Hofmannsthal und die Gedankenwelt Nietzsches* (Heidelberg, 1973), 53; Michael Hamburger, ed., Introduction to *Hugo von Hofmannsthal: Poems and Verse Plays* (New York, 1961), xvi.

One does not experience a "passing addiction" to vitalism any more than one experiences a passing addiction to life, and moreover, Hofmannsthal's work to resolve "the antimony between art and life" is apparent in his first publications—it does not wait for a "later solution." And finally, Nietzsche's greatest concern, though it is obviously lost on Hamburger, was to conceive of life, of living, as a phenomenon in need of style; and it was Nietzsche's great contribution to philosophy and aesthetics that after him art and philosophy became infused with life.

On matters of life in relation to art, as they were informed by Nietzsche during the last decade of the nineteenth century, but not necessarily exhausted or circumscribed by his philosophy, one should consider that not only Hofmannsthal but many who grew up in the *fin de siècle* felt enormously liberated by Nietzsche. With respect to Heym, Benn, Stadler, Zweig, Musil, Hesse, Rilke, Mann, Hofmannsthal, and George, Bruno Hillebrand explains, "They were all educated at schools and universities marked by the *Gründergeist* [founding spirit of the second Reich]: profit-minded and materialistic, utilitarian and optimistic, nationalistic. . . . Nietzsche, the European, embodied for them the liberation from such narrowness."[4] This liberating influence is seen in "Question," where the poet must ask the other if she does not long for a breath of life, for arms to bear her away from "this swamp of dreary, barren days."

Words themselves are not capable of breaking through to life, connecting with the soul. Words can be mere small talk, as in "Question," forever cut adrift from meaning, and there is always the danger that the poet, owing to his skill in using words, may be driven to confuse words with actual events and experiences. This particular problem Hofmannsthal addressed in "Secret of the World" ("Weltgeheimnis"). In eight terse strophes of three lines, a psychological history of the word moves from complete unity and knowledge to loss of knowledge among mortals and the conflation of knowledge and dream.

The deep well of the first strophe has knowledge, and at one time everyone was profound and silent, and everyone had knowledge. Without transition, however, and without being understood at its core, this knowledge now goes around "like magic words" in babble from mouth to mouth. The man who bends down to peer into the well momentarily comprehends the original knowledge but immediately loses it, though his contact with the source gives him the ability

4. Bruno Hillebrand, *Nietzsche und die deutsche Literatur* (Tübingen, 1978), 5.

to poetize: "And spoke confusedly and sang a song—." The next to look into the well is a child who becomes entranced; this child grows up without self-awareness and becomes a woman who is loved. It is love that strikes a fleeting link with the original knowledge of the well:

> How love brings deep tiding!—
> She receives vague intuitions
> In her kisses deep admonitions.
> (KA, I, 43)

The child's initial encounter with the source leaves her without self, but with the ability to regain something of the source through love. Hofmannsthal concludes with her, no other persons are mentioned in the last two strophes, but what the woman intuited (*geahnt*),

> It lies within our words,
> Such does the beggar's foot tread the pebble,
> That is the prison of a gem.

The poet heightens this image by revising the refrain:

> The deep well surely knows it,
> Once however everyone knew,
> Now a dream twitches around in a circle.

The loss of self extends now to everyone and everything, since the babble of words can no longer penetrate to the ground of the source. At best the poet is able to patch together a song from his confusion, or a little girl might become enrapt and surrender later on to the mysteries of love, but we are only able to come as close to the source as the beggar's foot to the gem it cannot comprehend, or recognize.

At the source, where all shared knowledge without speaking, there was unity and common knowledge. Hofmannsthal provides no transition from this source to the sudden precipitation of mankind into a state of babbling and incomprehension, after which only modest approaches can be made to the source through the medium of language. The "magic words" suddenly appear and now only the deep well has knowledge, while the rest of us stagger around in a dream. We have lost our depth ("Einst waren alle tief und stumm") and have become alienated from the source, but impulses from the source do reach us, however feebly, in the guise of words (confused speech, song, intuitions, admonitions provided by emotional experiences, etc.). This statement is not nearly as pessimistic as it sounds when analyzed, when criticism has been applied, since the message itself survives in the form of a poem bearing the title "Secret of the World." It is Hofmannsthal's understanding that this "secret" is not to be conveyed through cognition, and that the secret can at best be broached through poetry.

In his *ad me ipsum* notes to "Secret," Hofmannsthal spoke of "an ambivalent state between preexistence and life," in which individuals may come into selfhood. This gaining or coming into selfhood, according to his notes, was the motif of two major poems: "Guiding thought: Higher life must be the heightening of the self, received by rising up to what is proper, what is authentic (symbol: 'Dream of Great Magic' / 'The Deep Well'); it must set in as proper fulfillment of destiny, not as dream or trance" (*KA*, I, 219). In "Secret" the deep well symbolizes the individual self (*Ich*), which is the goal of man's striving and is also the undifferentiated source, a fact that Hofmannsthal underscores by beginning and concluding with "The deep well surely knows it." All intervening strophes, however, deal with the human consequences of babble and express potential, not apprehension of authenticity through language.

An additional dimension of the poet's consciousness of the lethargy or inertia of words emerges forcefully in "The Sin of Life" ("Sünde des Lebens"). Words are not only opaque, they are frequently rampant, out of control. The state of being that is "out of control" arises from our efforts to exert control, to wrest order from chaos using language to justify our position. In notes concerning "The Sin of Life" Hofmannsthal explained that he was working on a "'philosophical' but not didactic poem depicting the idea that no human could tolerate life if he could see through the conditions, disastrous consequences and vast responsibilities everyone must endure" (*KA*, I, 129). Our ability to tolerate life is based on the perception of the ego and our notion of identity, which rescues us from the chaotic nonself of phenomena. Hofmannsthal's "philosophical" approach is reminiscent of Schopenhauer's *principium individuationis*, from *The World as Will and Representation*, and also of Nietzsche's elaboration on the concept as an analog of the Apollinian principle in *The Birth of Tragedy*.

The poet of "The Sin of Life" has experienced a sort of revelation, so that in apocalyptic terms he exclaims:

> I have beheld the crime of life!
> I saw the germ of death that sprouts from life,
> The sea of guilt that flows from life,
> I saw the flood of sin burning,
> That we unwittingly commit

> Because we did not understand others,
> Because others do not understand us.
>   (*KA*, I, 14)

Given this knowledge of the conflation of life and death, of the guilt arising from living and the unwitting manner in which we inflict injury upon one another, the poet wishes his message could fly from house to house, "Piercingly through the roar of routine, / Awaken the world from its reeling" (*KA*, I, 15). The message is couched in the form of questions posed to various representatives of society, making "The Sin of Life" Hofmannsthal's longest published poem. The invoice of persons who are shocked from their complacency is suggestive of their capacity to deceive and be deceived; they are the guardians of meaning.

The first individual addressed by Hofmannsthal's apocalyptic "madman" is the poet, and the warning or admonition to him assumes thirty-four lines, far more than are devoted to the newlywed husband, rich man, priest, judge, and finally, to mankind.[5] The general atmosphere of the warnings is one of transvaluation, as seen for example in this strophe addressed to the judge:

> Judge, before you broke the staff
> Did not a voice speak within you:
> "Is the good then not the bad?
> Is injustice then not just?"
>   (*KA*, I, 17)

I am most concerned about the critique of the poet, however, since the poet ranks first among the practitioners of language gone rampant.

The poet is introduced wearing a crown of laurels, yet he is addressed as the "deceived deceiver." His mission of interpreting life and "redeeming the dreamy striving" in his own heart is called into question. Using a series of biting, rhetorical questions the poet is called to account: Is he even capable of understanding yesterday's thought; can he still feel last night's dream; does he understand why his soul weeps? In reality, "You have inklings, fancies, seeming things,— / Oh rather do not speak" (*KA*, I, 15). The poet is exhorted to remain silent, because as soon as his teeming intellect has posed

---

5. I use this term because Nietzsche's "madman" bearing a lantern during broad daylight, who has come to announce the death of God, speaks in a similar spirit. See *The Gay Science*, No. 125, in *Werke*, II, 126–28.

another structure into the world, the structure ceases to be true, and "You can hold it no longer, / You know not its lethal powers." These "lethal powers" put forth by the poet are then described in a separate strophe. Hofmannsthal uses irregular lines, dashes, ellipsis points, chorus-like strophes, and broken-line divisions between major "roles" in the poem to signify the confusion of language, and to steer clear of the mistakes in reasoning that he attributes to others who believe they have apprehended the whole when actually they are stumbling blindly.

The following two strophes conclude the admonition to the poet, and by reproducing them here in their entirety we can form a better picture of what Hofmannsthal intended.

> —Endless circles
> draws the quiet,
> Immortal word,
> On and on:—
>
> How it is interpreted, thousand-fold,
> Guides the world like a will 'o the wisp,
> With flattery deluding souls,
> In frenzy destroying souls,
> Eternally changing its form,
> Plunging forward through the ages,
> Appreciated, echoed,
> Heaving soulless and floating on,
> Staggering ever not understood,
> Ceaseless without rest or peace,
> Your mind's damned child,
> Immortal like you!
> - - - - - - - - - - - - - - - - - -
> - - - - - - - - - - - - - - - - - -
>
> (KA, I, 15–16)

The infinite circles described by the word are insidious, and the word itself is quiet (*leise*) and immortal; that is, it assumes a life of its own once the poet makes it current. The poet has no control over the poem because the word, immortal, returns to its eternal convolutions. The poet is not able to hold his words; as soon as they are discharged they have escaped his comprehension and principle of individuation, becoming his mind's "damned child." The eternal mutations of the word, its power to delude, flatter, destroy, gain veneration, and remain forever un-understood (*unverstanden*) make it sovereign and completely indifferent to man, its "father." Hofmannsthal explained that his poem was philosophical but not didactic, thereby indicating that he, at least, was not about to prescribe regulations governing poetry in the light of his insight. The poet's fate is to be superseded by his poem, and interpretation (*deuten, gedeutet*) as it is attributed to the poet (line 40) and to the poet's word (line 58) is revealed as a feeble strategy to exert control.

A milder expression of losing control in the face of poetry can be found in the brief poem "Where little cliffs, little pine trees" ("Wo kleine Felsen, kleine Fichten"). Hofmannsthal profiles the cliffs and trees against an open sky, and explains that from this perspective it is possible to see

> How we, drunk with poems,
> Childishly wander narrow paths.
> Are not we above all others
> The untouched children after all?
> Are not the boys less so,
> And the girls, those others?
> Are they true in their games,
> Those others, those many?
>
> (*KA*, I, 66)

Those who are sophisticated and learned, *e.g.*, the poets and the aesthetes drunk with poetry, may be more innocent than the children whose games are true. There is a suggestion that poetry allows us to walk childishly along narrow paths, so that the world does not touch us. If we transfer the unperceived chaos of "The Sin of Life" to this concept, it is possible to see why Hofmannsthal grants innocence to the word users.

Any attempt to interpret or read the world results in a retreat to an isolated position, to a perspective from which the world (life, longing, experience) is contained in a meditation or a poem. Even the boldest effort to countenance reality, or to fathom life by seeing through the veil of Maya, will result in a text designed to provide momentary safety and rescue from the chaotic worlding in which we are caught up. These texts, though we may be drunk on them, are the narrow paths to which our feet must cling. Poetry, insofar as it represents an effort, a striving, a working to render experience into text, is a practice of innocents. Less innocent, then, are the actual children whose games are plugged into the worlding, for children do not approach the world rationally, and therefore do not use language defensively.

In Hofmannsthal's *The Letter of Lord Chandos*, Chandos is supposed to have stopped writing "because I have completely lost the ability to think or to speak about something coherently [*zusammenhängend*]." [6] The predicament of Lord Chandos is close to the one suggested by Hofmannsthal in his notes to "The Sin of Life," *i.e.*, someone has seen through the conditions and manifold relationships of life, and is in danger of losing himself. Chandos explains that he became unable to tolerate gossip, local news, small talk, because "my mind compelled me to examine in uncanny proximity all the things that occurred in such conversation . . . I was no longer able to comprehend them with the simplifying gaze of habit" (*Prosa II*, 13). Language no longer subjected by the principle of individuation, and suitably restrained by convention, takes on a life of its own.

Each time Chandos experiences something without filtering it through the logic of grammar, without letting appearances establish themselves as authoritative, he feels so trapped that he has to rush outdoors into the open. Hofmannsthal is not necessarily criticizing language for its limits so much as he is trying to articulate the difficulty of having to maintain his presence in and through a language incommensurate with the force of experience: "For it is something totally unnamed and most likely also unnameable that conveys itself to me in such moments, some kind of appearance that fills up my everyday environment with an overflowing tide of higher life, like filling a vessel" (*Prosa II*, 14). Higher life, or more intensive life, manifests itself in the zone that breaks down text. Chandos is clearly not served by a language that reduces his presence to textuality when he is keenly, painfully aware that he himself is out of context.

When Chandos enters into the experiences of life, he confesses that "everything was in me . . . I bore it within me . . . but it was more, it was more divine, more animalistic; and it was presence, the fullest most sublime presence" (*Prosa II*, 15). In refusing to let words control his experience, Chandos succumbs to the control that words can only exert when they are momentarily detached from the principle of individuation and no longer contribute to a false, insular presence as in the everyday. He is able to experience life in its manifold forms from insect to rodent to human, a phenomenon he describes as "much more and much less than sympathy: a prodigious participating, a flowing over into those creatures or a feeling that a fluidum of life and death, of dreaming and waking flowed over into them for a moment" (*Prosa II*, 15). Hofmannsthal does not portray Chandos as a

6. Hofmannsthal, "Ein Brief [des Lord Chandos]," in *Hugo von Hofmannsthal: Gesammelte Werke in Einzelausgaben. Prosa II*, ed. Herbert Steiner (Frankfurt, 1952–59), Vol. V, Pt. 2, p. 11. Hereinafter cited parenthetically in the text as *Prosa II*.

stammering paralytic, nor as an ascetic who has made denial his lot in life as a result of having recognized language's deficiencies.

It is the exterior life of routine that Chandos neglects or merely fulfills according to habit, while he has become absorbed in the experience of life in the closest, rawest sense, where life itself takes control of language and seems to divorce it from existence. Hans Steffen alludes to this experience using Schopenhauer's terms, by explaining that the early Chandos strives for knowledge as the individual knowing subject, while the later Chandos is characterized no longer in terms of himself because he stands in direct relation to living.[7] This standing in direct relationship to living is, once again, similar to the condition Hofmannsthal described in "The Sin of Life," where the word becomes a marauding force of its own, the "damned child" of the poet. Just as in that poem the poet is exhorted to remain silent, Chandos too explains that he will no longer write, for his language has become one "in which mute things speak to me, and in which I perhaps will have to answer for myself someday, from the grave, before an unknown judge" (*Prosa II*, 19–20).

On one end of the poet-poem relationship words remain small talk and are incapable of striking a link between the soul, as the source or abode of life, and the outer life. On the other end, words can become autonomous—they are unleashed upon the world in such a way that the poet's consternation would have him withdraw into silence. In "The Sin of Life" the poet is admonished because he remains unaware of the insidious nature of his product; his words posit order and harmony where none exists, and Hofmannsthal tells us the poet, and the others, would surely perish if they could truly stand in the world without illusions. Lord Chandos, meanwhile, prefers to keep alive his private, unnameable link to the world, foregoing the outer life and listening to the language of things that do not speak to others. Still another dimension of the language/life interval treats the beautiful effect that language achieves, such that conditions in the world are idealized.

This idealizing process Hofmannsthal criticized in 1892 in "Prologue" ("Prolog"), a poem he read at a charity concert for the mountain community of Strobl. The first twenty-nine lines of the poem are dedicated to "our Strobl," *i.e.,* they describe what the community means in aesthetic terms to those who sojourn there in the summers.

---

7. Hans Steffen, "Schopenhauer, Nietzsche, und die Dichtung Hofmannsthals," in *Nietzsche. Werk und Wirkungen,* ed. Hans Steffen (Göttingen, 1974), 82.

Charming nature imagery abounds—the community is animated by colorful summer fashions, the laughing of children, the splashing music of fountains, and the fragrance of blossoms. It is clear that this Strobl is a place of escape,

> But there is yet another
> Not a sunny summer home,
> Colorful and laughter filled
> No, an everyday place, the home
> Of a total human life.
>
> (*KA*, I, 34–35)

Having thus divided his meditation on Strobl into the visitor's and the native's perspectives, Hofmannsthal uncovers the living Strobl by challenging the aesthetic with matter-of-fact values.

The real reason the gathering has assembled to come to the community's assistance, Hofmannsthal maintains, is the abiding Strobl not usually visible to the vacationer.

> What has summoned us here today
> Is the Strobl of all those
> Who stay always, when we go,
> Who do not look for the enigmatic
> Blue beauty of this water,
> Look not for fragrance and grace
> But instead to the pitiful
> Growth of their thin grain
> To the fruit of small gardens
> To the sustenance of their life;
> Who fear the wild and beautiful
> Storm because it could cast
> Sparks into dry haylofts;
> To whom this church tower bell,
> For us a gentle evening tolling
> On the lake, full of mood
> And poetic effect, means instead:
> Marriage, baptism and death.
>
> (*KA*, I, 35)

In the realm of nature those who are linked to nature by their dependence must necessarily see their own immediate needs reflected in the progress of their crops, and there is no time for idealization of phenomena that could make or break the people. Especially effective is Hofmannsthal's deconstruction of the romantic tolling bell; it contributes so easily, so readily to the visitor's flight of imagination, suggesting perhaps peace, serenity, constancy, homey simplicity, whereas it too has a hand in life. Marriage, baptism, death are all observed by the tolling of the bell and certainly understood as markers of these phenomena by the true inhabitants, who are pulled into living when they hear the bell, as opposed to being transported to an aesthetic playground of nostalgia and private bliss. The bell rings within the natural, living realm, as if nature itself were the hands that tug the rope to produce the sound, and the true inhabitants do not choose what they hear.

The distinction between beauty and life was approached in "Prologue" within the context of society versus nature, a familiar romantic paradigm popular among writers since Goethe's *The Sorrows of Young Werther* (1774) or even earlier, harking back to Rousseau's influence on the eighteenth century. But Hofmannsthal was not exalting nature for its own sake, elevating it, urging us to imitate it; instead, he used the lives of those living in nature to reveal the poverty of aesthetic perception. Beauty is one thing, and life, nature, and art are not circumscribed by beauty.

Hofmannsthal participated in 1893 in a performance of living paintings; individuals dressed the part of figures from paintings, and assembled themselves accordingly. Afterward, the individuals passed by in procession (*KA*, I, 199). Hofmannsthal delivered the prologue and epilogue for this event, entitled "Prologue and Epilogue to the Living Paintings" ("Prolog und Epilog zu den lebenden Bildern"). In itself the event must have fascinated Hofmannsthal, who also portrayed a character, because the normally plastic medium of painting was animated both dramatically, in the "coming to life" and procession of the figures, and lyrically, by Hofmannsthal's poetic accompaniment. The poem is very much in the spirit of translating the static into the dynamic, and it explores the interval between aesthetic effect and living.

In the prologue Hofmannsthal introduces a view of art reminiscent in many ways of Wilhelm Heinrich Wackenroder's influential writings from the 1790s. The viewing of artworks, paintings in particular, should not be done in a profane manner, *i.e.*, when we enter a museum we are entering a church or a temple, and the proper state of mind is reverence, not curiosity. The momentum of the everyday must not be carried into one's experience of the paintings, or the wondrous, divine "language" of art, transmitted as a gift to the painter and through his painting to us, will not emerge.[8] This is according to Wackenroder, who is justifiably regarded in the history of letters as an early spokesman for the alienated artist. The opening lines of the prologue are set off from the remaining forty lines, which are the body of the prologue:

> Not as though before a stage should you
> Sit here expectantly: wild beauty will not
> Play quivering notes upon your soul's strings
> With fingers feverish and stimulating.
> Here matters the tiny art that does not seize,
> That only willingly seized can be.
>
> (*KA,* I, 38)

Beauty is described as wild and capable of exciting passions; play-goers might expect to be stimulated, moved, but these are passive operations visited upon "expectant" viewers. Hofmannsthal hopes the viewers of the living paintings will be receptive to the tiny art ("hier gilt's der kleinen Kunst") that can only be comprehended when it gives itself.

The epilogue clarifies the nature of this art. Describing the procession of figures while he is reading the epilogue, Hofmannsthal asks, "Are they silent mortals, are they moving dolls?" (*KA,* I, 39). The nature of the figures is complicated because they have been liberated from the plastic medium, "Yet what each one is, that it is totally; / Totally the breathing symbol *of one* mood" (*KA,* I, 40). The "breathing symbol" and the value of the symbol in general, the question of totality and unity in one mood, surpass the mere appearance and obtrusiveness of wild beauty. This notion is underscored at the conclusion of the strophe when the poet insists that beauty resides in orchids, the awe-inspiring night, in wild forests and green lakes, while beauty that is charged with soul ("durchseelte Schönheit") goes by the name of art.

The deception practiced by the appearance of beauty has the effect of insulating us from the events of life, as suggested in the aesthetic perceptions of "Prologue," when they are held up against the perceptions of the common inhabitants. The appearance of beauty makes visitors of us, and as visitors, the place in which we sojourn conforms to our fleeting, self-indulgent needs. In "Prologue to the Living Paint-

8. Wilhelm Heinrich Wackenroder, *Confessions and Fantasies,* trans., annotated by Mary Hurst Schubert (University Park, Pa., 1971), 125–26, 118.

ings," on the other hand, the painting-figures that are brought to life are "Totally the breathing symbol *of one* mood." These figures are a totality because they possess life (breath, soul) and symbolize oneness of mood. The symbol is not synonymous with an appearance—it does not represent a substitution, a reflection, a part of the essence, but the essence itself.

"Dialogue on Poems" ("Das Gespräch über Gedichte"), a short theoretical work from the year 1903, elaborates Hofmannsthal's position on the symbol. Clemens opines that poetry (*Poesie*) is not the same as language: "It is full of images and symbols. It posits one thing for the other."[9] This remark brings forth a spirited rejoinder from Gabriel: "Never does poetry posit one thing for another, for it is precisely poetry that strives feverishly to posit the thing itself, with an energy quite different than blunt every day speech, with a magic power quite different than the weakling terminology of science" (*Prosa II*, 84). The unity of symbol and thing, symbol and event, symbol and experience is a condition of nature "which has no other means to comprehend us ["uns zu fassen"], to pull us to it, than this enchantment. It is the embodiment of symbols that compel us. It is what our body is, and our body is what it is" (*Prosa II*, 89).

In his recent book on Hofmannsthal, Benjamin Bennett lends a succinct expression to the "magic" of poetry as Hofmannsthal perceived it: "The magic of poetry is not an elevation of the soul above normal existence, but the revelation of what is always inherent *in* our existence."[10] I particularly favor this wording because it makes clear that poetry, no more so than symbol, is not supposed to transcend, and whenever we attempt to posit one thing for another, we are in fact attempting to transcend a thing and to take up residence in another thing somewhere else. Nature's body is our body, its language is our language emerging through symbols, in very much the same way that Nietzsche contends in *The Birth of Tragedy* that the lyricist joins with nature and articulates primal unity using the lyricist as a nonsubjective medium. The unity of lyricist and reality, or Nietzsche's

9. The title of the essay and its spirit hark back to Friedrich Schlegel's influential *Dialogue on Poetry* (1800), in which different characters articulate the romantic view of art by symphilosophizing (*symphilosophieren*). See the translation and elaboration of same by Ernst Behler and Roman Struc, *Dialogue on Poetry and Literary Aphorisms* (University Park, Pa., 1968); Hofmannsthal, *Prosa II*, 84.

10. Benjamin Bennett, *Hugo von Hofmannsthal: The Theaters of Consciousness* (Cambridge, Eng., 1988), 27–28.

primal unity, is what led him in the same chapter of *Tragedy* to proclaim that "only as an *aesthetic phenomenon* is existence and the world
eternally *justified*" (I, 37–40).

It is clear that language which is successful only in providing the
appearance of beauty is failed speech, inauthentic expression that
posits one thing for another. Matters are quite different, however,
when the thing is symbolized and apprehended in its essence, as is
the case in Hofmannsthal's high conception of art. Aestheticism is the
false mood whereby beautiful appearance is perceived to be sustaining for the individual, while art is the enacting of the genuine mood
in which individual and all (nature) speak together by use of the common language.

Meyer-Wendt describes Hofmannsthal's understanding of aestheticism as a mood characterized by "an overgrown sensitivity and the
observance of the past through artistic media, resulting in being in
love with stylized life, i.e., with the observance of a given image of
life and not in life itself." [11] Life as style only, or life as style primarily,
can never be consummated life because style fascinates us at the expense of life; it is easier, and it is *of our making* and therefore unequivocally allied with us against the contingencies and mysteries of life
itself. The symbol that posits one thing for another, like the poem that
pretends to be its own life and *raison d'être* by using beautiful symbols,
has not gone the difficult and authentic route of extracting the marrow from each thing. Only when each thing has been articulated
in its "propriety" (Latin *proprium*, "sein Eigenstes") has poetry done
its work. [12]

Beyond the insidious power of marauding words detailed in "The
Sin of Life" there is a power inherent in words that succeed in extracting the essence from things. This power, in itself neither good nor
bad, seems to explain why Hofmannsthal published his poems for ten
years without becoming cynical, without burning out, despite the fact
that his earliest poetic writing was animated by criticism of sanctimo-
nious art. "Ballad of the Outer Life" ("Ballade des äusseren Lebens")
is a prime example of the meaning residing in the word, though in
this poem of twenty-two lines the poet takes us to the very brink
of nonmeaning, to the brink of nihilism before he pulls himself and
us out.

11. Meyer-Wendt, *Der frühe Hofmannsthal*, 81.
12. Hofmannsthal, *Dialogue on Poems*, in *Prosa II*, 84. Webster's 3rd unabridged dic-
tionary offers "true nature" as one obsolete usage of *propriety*, and another approxima-
tion to Hofmannsthal's *Eigenstes* can be found in the etymology of *property*.

"Ballad" was written around 1894, some seven or eight years before the famous "Chandos Letter" that roughly coincides with the falling off of Hofmannsthal's lyrical productivity. The poem's mood is well summarized in the first strophe:

> And children grow up with deep eyes,
> That know of nothing, grow up and die,
> And all people go their ways.
>
> *(KA,* I, 44)

The "And" beginning this poem is already ominous; things have always been this way, and the poem suggests, not a fresh start, but merely a continuation, since wherever it "breaks in" it leaves the cycle unbroken. The second through fifth strophes, all three-liners, offer similar depressing observations: Fruits ripen and rot; winds blow and words get tossed around while we vacillate between excitement and weariness; roads stretch through the fields punctuated by villages showing signs of life and signs of death. Their multiplicity, their very presence is baffling, and the poet cannot fathom the everyday changes from laughter to weeping to dying.

> What good is all of this and these games,
> To us who are big and eternally alone anyway
> And wandering never search for any goals?
>
> What good is it to have seen much of these things?
> And yet, he who says "evening" says much,
> A word from which deep thought and sadness run
>
> Like heavy honey from the comb.
>
> *(KA,* I, 44)

The turning within the meditation takes place in the word "evening" because evening is an event central to every life. In his notes to himself Hofmannsthal mentioned Sappho, Augustine, and Novalis as sources for the special significance of evening *(KA,* I, 224–25). For our purposes, Hofmannsthal's expressed view of evening as "fulfillment, something millenarian" will suffice *(KA,* I, 224).

Juxtaposition of life and death serves to unify semantically the inexorable parade of events beginning with the words "And children." On one end there is life, and intervening are the meaningless games, the laughter and weeping, crowned on the other end by death. But we are big now, protests the poet, and eternally alone and wandering without goals, so that these games and our having seen much of this brief intervening life appear to be in vain. The poet reverses himself by recognizing that the one who says "evening" has said much; to say "evening" is to have lived long and to have one's affairs in order at the evening of one's life; there is fulfillment just as after an honest day's work there is fulfillment and return to the hearth.

The one who *says* "evening," who speaks the word, has recognized his time and is therefore entitled to the powers of that word. Deep thought and sadness flow like thick honey from the word; there is ripeness, consummation of life such that life's essence runs and spills forth, no longer contained by the hollow comb that cannot survive as the essence of life, in any case, but only as its containment. The poet waits until the final strophe to sound a positive note, as if to say that the consummation of a life lies, not in how one perceives life, but in the fact that one grows old and looks back upon a life such that there can be an evening. How the life appears to us is not of crucial importance. Having lived it, on the other hand, and having maintained the presence to utter the word "evening" and thereby release its rewarding powers, means everything.

The power of the word may of course remain unknown to us, as was the case in the poet's warning to the poet in "The Sin of Life." Other instances in which Hofmannsthal explored the effect words have on our lives, without our necessarily being aware, occur in his epigrams, all of which deal with language. "Words" ("Worte") appears very straightforward:

> There are some words that hit like clubs. But some
> You swallow like hooks and swim on and don't know it
> yet.
>
> (*KA*, I, 87)

Given enough line, the unsuspecting fish will swim away until the line becomes taut and the fish is jerked out of its element, where it will perish or, perhaps, be thrown back. The words that leave their mark, bruising and punishing, at least can be seen from a distance; such words could be dodged, ostensibly, or somehow parried, and even if they manage to strike, there is always the small consolation that the bruise will heal.

Not so with the word-hooks that are unwittingly swallowed, however, for we have taken the bait and are prepared to run until we are out of line. The word-hooks give us no knowledge of our fate; once we are jerked out of our element, say, our everyday routine, our belief in someone or something, we are capable only of knowing that we got hooked somewhere back in time. It is also possible, pursuing Hofmannsthal's analogy, that we struck at the baited word-hook because we were hungry or in need, or because the bait seemed easy prey. Man's susceptibility to words is like the fish's reaction to bait—it goes for it instinctively, while man preys on words and ends up being dragged around, preyed upon by a superior power.

Another epigram expresses the idea of man being pulled around by words. "One's Own Language" ("Eigene Sprache") is the appropriately ambiguous title of this meditation:

> If language grew in your mouth, then the chain grew into
> your hand:
> Now pull the universe to you! Pull! Or else you will
> be dragged.
> (*KA*, I, 87)

"One's own language" in this sense is not one's so-called native language, or mother tongue, or one's particular idiom or usage—one's own language is the language of one's making, in the sense that a being makes itself in growing into its relation to the world. Decisive here is the *proprium* Hofmannsthal wants the poet to extract from every thing.

German *eigen, das Eigene,* and its derivatives play a major role in Heidegger's *Being and Time,* with a meaning similar to Hofmannsthal's. Heidegger's translators use such terms as "ownmost," "most its own," and "authentic" for rendering variations of *eigen.*[13] A thing's property, its essence, is unique to itself and therefore occupies a privileged place in the world, one not occupied by any other thing. Hofmannsthal did not trust everyday language or the language of science to apprehend the property of a thing, and on closer consideration, it has to remain one of the poet's vital functions to ascertain, through symbol or otherwise, what is in the world. No one else has *time* in the sense that the poet shares time and makes time.

The words that grow within one's mouth can be swallowed or spoken; they can be used to take, as one takes nourishment or medicine, and they can be used to give, as one gives encouragement or abuse. This is why the poet insists that a conditional is operative here; if it is such with words, then understand that a chain is likewise placed into

---

13. Martin Heidegger, *Being and Time,* trans. John Macquarrie and Edward Robinson (New York, 1962), 312, 349, 508.

your hand, a chain that anchors you to the universe just as surely as the words that are your orientation, your yes and no. Given this grounding or anchoring by the force of word and chain (this can also be a word-chain, of course, set in motion by the first word), if one does not pull with all his might, the universe will simply drag him along. There is a titanism here, both in the attitude of affirmation that would enable one to pull the universe and in the notion that one's language is one's strength, one's very life, one's only virtue, and is in direct proximity to the universe.

There is also optimism in this statement. Yes, it is the human's fate to be grounded in the world, but this grounding is not arbitrary. Hofmannsthal is saying that if language grows in us, the fulfillment of the condition is that we also have grounding, *i.e.*, the chain in the hand. The chain is not binding us in any sense, because language sets the bond (ground) in motion, and because Hofmannsthal clearly uses the accusative case to signal placement of the chain *into* the hand subsequent to language consciousness ("so wuchs in die Hand Dir die Kette"). The unity of language and chain constitute a plus.

The "if" clause of the conditional requires illumination. Language, one's own and innermost essence, grows in the mouth, while the mouth is the mechanism by which language will be used. Language without mouth is inconceivable or, at least, incomplete. The poet easily could have written "if language grew in your mind," but of course that would disrupt the ascent of concrete images required to articulate the nature of language. Language is indeed a thing of the mind, but its best friend and closest ally is the mouth, which will produce speech. The "if" could be read as a teleological negative: *If* it is man's curse to suffer the growing of language in his mouth, *then at least* something can be done with it, namely, one can pull the universe, use language to create one's self, to situate one's self and one's own (one's *proprium*) in the universe. Allowing oneself to be dragged by the universe at the other end of the chain would amount to swallowing one's own, one's own language and self—it would amount to standing in the world in abject silence.

Or even worse, swallowing one's own, one's potential, instead of expressing that potential of selfhood, would be to suffer the paralyzing nausea that Zarathustra beholds in the face of the writhing shepherd: The shepherd is thrashing about on the ground with a thick black snake lodged in his throat, and Zarathustra cannot extract the serpent by pulling with *his* hands. Only Zarathustra's lifesaving advice to bite off the snake's head, enabling the shepherd to spit it forth, restores the shepherd to the living and transforms him to the super-living. Zarathustra's words are encouragement and *command;* they are uttered aggressively in a situation that is desperate beyond compre-hension and that calls for action. The proper action-intervention, in this case, is precipitated by language. Zarathustra must first conceive a plan after failing to tug the snake from the shepherd's throat, and once conceived, that plan, amounting to certain words strategically linked in a flash of insight, has to be transmitted from the speaker and comprehended by the listener. The reader of this passage is im-pressed by the spell Nietzsche is able to create, as though temporarily paralyzing the reader along with the shepherd. The breaking of the spell owes to the proper, appropriate (authentic) use of language, and language, having done its work, is then superseded by the uncanny laughter of the shepherd once he is delivered from his anguish. This powerful, liberating laughter is articulation on a higher plain than mortals are able to achieve, and it haunts Zarathustra-Nietzsche.

A final epigram entitled "Poets and Present" ("Dichter und Gegen-wart") illuminates the power of words by exploring the poet's relation to time.

> "We are your wing, oh time, and hold you above chaos.
> But, confused time, are we also talons that bear you?"
> "Comfort yourselves, This has ever been. And shudder that
> you are chosen—:
> The shuddering were always wing and talon to me like
> you."
> (*KA*, I, 86)

The poets who address time establish the present, *i.e.,* they differen-tiate among past, present, and future by suspending time above chaos and rescuing it from oblivion. What the poets must question, however, is the manner in which time holds itself aloft. It would be acceptable to the poet if he had to serve only as the wings of time, for this suggests an organic relationship; time, otherwise immobile and in danger of becoming swallowed by chaos, would not escape flux if not for the wings attached to its shoulders. The poet does not seem to resent time for requiring his effort to remain aloft and to therefore function as a marker, as the present. A second version of this epigram was published years later under a new title, "The Poets and Time" ("Die Dichter und die Zeit"): "We are your wing, oh time, but we are not the talon that bears you! / Or do you demand so much: wing and talon at once?" (*KA*, I, 86, 361–62).

However, the poet justifiably suggests that time must be confused; the poet is not supposed to bear it aloft, a dead weight in his talons like some great eagle. This implies a separation between poet and time, with time serving as the force of gravity passively suspended from the eagle's claws. Time must do more for itself in order to remain above chaos. From the poet's point of view, time is too heavy, and the poet's flight too delicate. The proverbial "winged time" suggests some alleviation of the poet's strain, but time borne by the claws of eagles poses a problem: The eagle must land at some point and would have to release its grip on time, while winged time could stay aloft confident of the poet's blessing in his less demanding relationship to time. Moreover, the grasp of claws could weaken, such that time would fall into the abyss.

Despite the poet's motivation for addressing time as confused, and his reluctance to hold time in his talons, time ordains that both wing and claw have always been a factor and that the poet's best recourse is to shudder, to be in awe of this relationship, for poets are the chosen ones. Those who are capable of awe, capable of the "fear and trembling" à la Kierkegaard, are, like the poets, the ones employed by time to hold it aloft. This tells us more about time than about the poets, or perhaps, *what* it tells us about time reflects on the virtues of the poets.

The poets should comfort themselves—nothing is amiss in this relationship, and not bewilderment but awe is the proper response. Those capable of awe, of shuddering, of fear and trembling, are those who would go to such lengths as to serve time both as its wings and its skyhook. The nature of time is lethargic, it threatens at every turn to fall back into chaos, into prehistory, into prelanguage. Those who brought time into the world in demonstrable form, introducing the dimensions of time and contributing to the all-important present, are none other than the poets and the priests, who have always been stricken by awe, who have always been the shuddering ones. Time itself can only call out to the poets and reinforce their dialogue by assuring him, the poet, that his instrumentality has been responsible all along for keeping time aloft. Time is not proud, not instrumental, but it has always earned the veneration of the special keepers of time, the story and hi-story tellers, who are truly chosen. The poets will fade, will fail, if time fades and is allowed to fall back. Therefore the bearing of time in any mode, whether by wing or by claw, whether it wills or wills not to soar, is an operation linked every bit as closely as the language/mouth, hand/chain nexus of "One's Own Language."[14]

Hofmannsthal was surely aware of the venerable literary history behind *das Schaudern* as a concept. In *Faust*, Part 2, Mephistopheles has provided Faust with the means to descend to the Mothers, a most dangerous journey beyond all human bounds and imagination. When Faust hears the word "mothers," he quakes and immediately confesses that the sound of the word strikes him with dread. Mephistopheles urges him on by challenging him to continue to explore the unexplored in the spirit of the original wager, in which Faust promised never to rest, and never to say to any moment or experience: Stay! thou art so fair![15] Faust swears to forfeit his very life if he ever surrenders to the moment, and he alludes specifically to time by claiming, "The clock may stop, the hands may freeze, / My time would be at end!" (lines 1705–1706). Later, Mephistopheles appeals to this bravado and elicits another commitment to action: Faust will venture the journey to the nether realm of the Mothers, claiming,

> I sought my fortune not in petrifaction,
> The best part of humanity is awe;
> Just as the world makes precious all our senses,
> Man is moved, and awe is felt most deeply.
> (lines 6271–74)

Faust's journey to the Mothers lets even Mephistopheles wonder if Faust will be able to return, and having been among them he is driven to commit another dangerous act, that of clinging to the chimeric Helen as if to drag her into this world. He appeals to the Mothers to help him "rescue" Helen, which is tantamount to resurrecting her and giving flesh and blood to a ghost. At the end of Act 2 there is an explosion, the chimera dissolve, and Faust has to be carried away by Mephistopheles. Goethe wanted to underscore the *danger* involved in seizing and apprehending time actively, as opposed to merely subsisting. Faust is the one who lives dangerously. Generations before Nietzsche made "living dangerously" an existentialist buzzword, Goethe gave us the man of action par excellence; he throws himself into any danger for the sake of those glorious, fulfilled moments of

14. Chapter 7 gives a detailed reading of this epigram in the broader context of time in Hofmannsthal's poetic.

15. In German, line 1700 reads: "Verweile doch! du bist so schön!" (Johann Wolfgang von Goethe, *Faust: Der Tragödie erster und zweiter Teil*, ed. Erich Trunz [Munich, 1977], 57).

living on the precipice, living in awe. Hofmannsthal's insistence that poets serve as the suspenders of time, with nothing but quaking and trembling as their natural reward, is an epigrammatic articulation of Faust's great mission: In order to heighten feeling in and for the present and ultimately stand before time with a sense of awe, Faust journeys into the mythical-poetic past as though it were a physical dimension capable of inflicting bodily harm.

In the 1890s, the decade of his best lyrical work, Hofmannsthal did not allow his close knowledge of the working of language to dissuade him from publishing, and I agree with Katharina Mommsen who explains that the language-skeptical expressions are balanced by "an abundance of positive expressions and passages where Hofmannsthal-Loris is thoroughly aware of the early richness of his poetic language and praises it with gratitude and astonishment."[16] There were strong motivating circumstances operating during the *fin de siècle* that set the young poet on a diverging path, away from aestheticism and into the uncharted terrain of the philosophy of life.

The greatest of these background conditions has been suggested by Hermann Broch. There was a value vacuum in the art of the German-speaking lands at the end of the nineteenth century, and Nietzsche discovered it in Wagner, whom he diagnosed as the decadent "uncomposer," the free-stylist who thrived in the vacuum. But Hofmannsthal could not thrive in this absence of meaning: "The value vacuum of the world, affirmed by Wagner as the nourishing soil from which he drew his strength, was for Hofmannsthal by far the deepest anxiety of his life."[17] There is textual evidence to support Broch's claim.

For example, Hofmannsthal made the following notations in 1892 when he was reading Nietzsche's *On the Genealogy of Morals:* "Atmosphere: German self-conceit after 1870. . . . Possession: a pure concept of the creating artist and his secret relation to life . . . who actually invents values? Answer: those who speak."[18] Nietzsche was anything but a "value-neutral" thinker. For him, all questions of value were inextricably connected to the phenomenon life; ascending life has life-affirming values, descending or declining life has nihilistic values. Hofmannsthal even at the tender age of eighteen understood the artist's, specifically the poet's, role on the issue of values or value

16. Katharina Mommsen, "Loris und Nietzsche: Hofmannsthals *Gestern* und Frühe Gedichte in Neuerer Sicht," *German Life and Letters,* XXXIV (1980), 50.

17. Hermann Broch, *Hofmannsthal und seine Zeit* (Frankfurt, 1974), 111.

18. Hofmannsthal, in Hillebrand, *Nietzsche,* 82.

vacuum. The creating artist creates values, but in order for these values to amount to anything, to surpass the German "self-conceit" after its triumph over France in 1870–1871, the values cannot be a *creatio ex nihilo*—Hofmannsthal turned to life, turned to it and also attempted to turn it inside out, in his effort to find a legitimate source for values. Wherever his poetic language soars, it is always held close to the earth by the burden of time, the *present* to which the poet feels responsibility because he, with time, establishes the present.

3 ACTIONS

Language contributes to an insular existence by structuring the *principium individuationis* that keeps us functioning and keeps us apart from all things and all others. This necessary and laudable working of language, its everydayness, is a mere starting point as far as the poet is concerned. The poet's experience with language uncovers another dimension of language that is not always laudable, though it may indeed prove necessary, and that shadow of speech falls upon experience, casting over it a pall that cannot be penetrated. If words are allowed to stand as a buffer between the individual and the world, a phenomenal "out-there" is established to which we cannot gain access, in which we do not take part. There are dangers inherent in establishing an out-there through language.

To the extent that we do not take part in the out-there, we do not feel empathy or responsibility. On the contrary, divorcing ourselves from phenomena fosters a mentality of self-indulgence, of self-deception, such that we play with all things as though they were mere products randomly situated in the world for our entertainment, or perhaps to test our skills as "builders." Poets are constantly in danger of falling prey to their own gratuitous building, for in the poet the capacity for fleeing into language not only is a function of the everyday, where language is used defensively to insulate oneself, but also becomes a tool for wielding power. On closer examination, however, the poet does not wield anything but seeming power, for the condition of the poet when he indulges in language is one of paralysis of the will.

Perhaps Sartre said it best in his essay "What is Literature?" "Poets," he wrote, "are people who refuse to *use* language." By "use" Sartre does not mean that poets do not avail themselves of language but instead that poets do not approach language teleologically. The poet neither speaks, according to Sartre, nor does he remain silent. The speaking person stands "beyond words, at the object" whereas the poet stands "this side of words." For the speaker words are servants, but for the poet words remain in a wild state like things given in nature, every bit as natural as the growing grass and the trees.[1] Sartre's distinction between the speaker and the poet, or between the words of prose and the words of poetry, is useful in helping to establish Hofmannsthal's position on paralysis of the will.

The poet's "use" of words can never be identical with the speaker's use of words, insofar as the poet does not wield power over words such that he can shape them and bend them to his will, for instance in order to fashion a message, a doctrine, or an argument. It is indeed the case that poets frequently do not represent themselves as poets in Sartre's sense of the word, *i.e.*, poets can try to enlist words and force them to subscribe to a purpose, but here the poet would merely be a speaker, a failed poet. Sartre uses the reverse of this analogy to describe the prose writer/speaker who appears to have no purpose: He is not therefore a poet, but a writer who speaks without saying anything.[2] The poet who merely loves to build, and who builds gratuitously in order to dwell within his own word structures, is also a failed poet because he has attempted to harness words for his own use and entertainment. Where poetry is merely an extension of speaking or an ersatz for prose, we have a presence of will but an absence of poetry.

The poet as defined by Sartre has a special way with words based on a complete lack of exploitation, and his definition of the poet reminds one very much of Nietzsche's definition of the lyricist as medium in *The Birth of Tragedy* (chapter 5). According to Sartre words are not signposts for the poet; they do not pull him out of himself and hurl him out among the objects of the world. Instead, because he already stands outside, the poet regards words as a snare with which to capture a fleeting reality: "For him language is a mirror of the world and nothing more."[3] The poet's authentic access to the outside world, as opposed to the building of an outer world through use of speech (prose, speaking, failed poetry), appears therefore to require a suspension of the will in the same manner that Nietzsche's Dionysian lyricist has let go of the will in order to serve as the medium of the Primal Unity.

1. Jean-Paul Sartre, "What is Literature?" in *"What is Literature?" and Other Essays*, (Cambridge, Mass., 1988), 29.
2. *Ibid.*, 34.
3. *Ibid.*, 30.

In his essay "Gabriele d'Annunzio" (1893) Hofmannsthal described the few thousand writers scattered throughout Europe as the consciousness of their generation, and the editorial "we" of the following excerpt of course includes him: "We have nothing but a sentimental memory, a paralyzed will and the uncanny ability of doubling ourselves [*Selbstverdoppelung*]. We observe our life; prematurely we drain the chalice and still remain infinitely thirsty. For, as Bourget recently said so beautifully and sadly, the chalice that life holds out to us is cracked, and whereas the full drink might have intoxicated us, we will miss eternally what trickles down to the ground as we are drinking."[4]

The capacity to double or clone oneself, instead of growing into and possibly beyond oneself, suggests an existence that is a closed circuit. The circuit is closed because we merely observe life and are prone to sentimental observation, to nostalgia as opposed to engaging in the life that one would not be observing if one were living it. The above quotation, because it is prose and couched in the language of speaking, admirably fulfills the requirements of speech but not of poetry; Hofmannsthal's will is in evidence, and he uses it to convey his criticism of the modern person.

But the nature of this criticism deserves further scrutiny. If words have their own life, as Sartre suggests, and their own élan as well, the best we can do under the best circumstances as users of words, that is, as poets, is to cling to them for a time or snare "realities." When Hofmannsthal writes that we "drain the chalice" but remain thirsty, he implies that it is in the nature of life to be spilled, to be squandered, to slip through our fingers. Be that as it may, it is still incumbent upon the poet to live in an authentic relationship with language, for no one but the poet is capable of living "this side" of words. The cup may indeed be cracked, and this insight may indeed result in critical spoken judgments such as sentimental, paralyzed, beautiful, and sad, but Hofmannsthal clearly is not condoning the resignation of his age so much as he is trying to clear the air of a spellbinding aesthetic lethargy.

In an article on Nietzsche's influence on Hofmannsthal and the *fin de siècle* I argued that Nietzsche's philosophy cannot assume the same dimensions in Hofmannsthal's poetry that it assumed in the prose of writers such as Thomas Mann. For this reason, Nietzsche's influence

4. Hofmannsthal, "Gabriele d'Annunzio," in *Hugo von Hofmannsthal: Gesammelte Werke in Einzelausgaben. Prosa I*, ed. Herbert Steiner (Frankfurt, 1952–59) Vol. V, Pt. 1, p. 148. Hereinafter cited parenthetically in the text as *Prosa I*.

on Mann and other prose writers is more apparent, but it may well be less substantial.[5] Nietzsche had his agenda as a philosopher, and he was intent on being persuasive. Hofmannsthal, on the other hand, had no particular ax to grind, at least not in the poetry, and he was certainly not trying to convince anyone that he was a philosopher. The critical tone of the critical writings aside, it would appear that Hofmannsthal was content to let the will speak in parables.

Since the poet has no power over his words beyond the poem that he is "permitted" to create by virtue of suspending his will, the poet's success has to be measured in terms of the "fleeting realities" he is able to snare and, presumably, to display. For the poet must leave a record of his journey behind, and that record is most appropriately written in the language that does not speak but does not remain silent either, to use Sartre's evasive formulation. The less volition we ascribe to the poet, the more it will appear that poems are simply his traces. Like the tail of a comet the poet's words trail behind him, and though he is heedless of them once they are in the world, we are not. Paralysis of the will must in some measure apply to the poet as well, for his discourse must not assert itself with the force of persuasion, nor be animated by any spirit that is not in the spirit of the words. However, the poet's service to words includes the reflection or mirroring of their reality to his community, and it may well be that these poetic doses of reality are as much as a "speaking" public are able to bear.

Hofmannsthal was particularly concerned about paralysis of the will, and his information concerning the will derived in large measure from Goethe, Schopenhauer, and Nietzsche. But as Steffen correctly points out, Hofmannsthal was able to conceive of the will in his own terms because he read Nietzsche with Schopenhauer's eyes and vice versa.[6] This circumstance enabled Hofmannsthal to appreciate Schopenhauer without the rigidity of Nietzsche's antiromantic critique, which of course included a complete reappraisal of Schopenhauer's philosophy. The criticism traditionally leveled at the poet is that he is a dreamer, not a man of action, an aesthete whose eloquence seems to put the world in proper perspective. However, returning to Hofmannsthal's point that we merely observe life (*zuschauen*), we discover that adulation of life from a comfortable distance is a sign of modernity: "Today two things seem to be modern: the analysis of life and the escape from life" (*Prosa I*, 149). In either mode, whether by analy-

5. Adrian Del Caro, "Hofmannsthal as a Paradigm of Nietzschean Influence on the Austrian fin de siècle," *Modern Austrian Literature*, XXII (1989), 83.

6. Steffen, "Schopenhauer, Nietzsche, und die Dichtung Hofmannsthals," 85.

sis or by aesthetic retreat, or even if the analysis is conducted by means of aesthetic retreat, the will is paralyzed as a means for action and participation.

Analysis is closely linked to criticism, and both criticism and poetry for their own sake provide sufficient excitement, fulfillment, and sustenance to the modern intellect. This point Hofmannsthal illuminated by describing what he saw in d'Annunzio's fictional characters, namely, "an uncanny lack of will" and "that experiencing of life not as a chain of actions but as conditions instead" (*Prosa I*, 150). The consequence of lack of will was treated by Hofmannsthal in the epigram "One's Own Language"; one either pulls the universe on the chain in his hand, or one is dragged. A vicarious experience of life occurs when life is not embraced as a series of actions or deeds (*Handlungen*). Any action can bring forth a reaction, any deed, as Goethe put it, is a sort of misdeed that takes on an ethical momentum of its own. "The one who acts is always without conscience; no one has conscience but the reflective one."[7] But Goethe also justified the need for action in human affairs, as seen in the "Prologue in Heaven" of *Faust*; the Lord tells Mephistopheles (lines 340–44) that human activity is prone to subside, so that man becomes enamored of absolute calm. It is for this reason that the devil is given to man as a companion who incites him to take action.[8]

Hofmannsthal expressed his sympathy with Goethe's view quite clearly in "The Sin of Life." Toward the end of the poem, when mankind is being addressed following the illumination or sobering of society's leaders, we read:

> No one has an inkling of crimes he commits,
> Nor of his guilt, nor of his duty!
> Are you allowed to live when every step
> Effaces a thousand unknown lives,
> When you cannot think, cannot feel
> Without engaging in lies and seduction!
>
> (*KA*, I, 18)

Involvement in life becomes complicity in life, so that there is no innocence. Life's momentum is greater than the momentum of any single life form, moreover, so that individual man is not held up to an absolute ethical standard; it is man's best fate to become embroiled in

7. Johann Wolfgang von Goethe, *Maximen und Reflexionen*, in *Johann Wolfgang von Goethe. Werke. Hamburger Ausgabe in 14 Bänden*, ed. Erich Trunz (Munich, 1982), XII, 399.
8. Goethe, *Faust*, 18.

life, and what man knows, as the thinking animal, is not supposed to paralyze his limbs when the time for action comes.

Strength of will, strength of character are prerequisites to experiencing life as a chain of actions, for this chain or series is constantly transforming and calling for new measures, new strategies—the chain of actions pulls the universe to us because we accept the burden (or opportunity) of working with the consequences of what we set in motion.

Not so with the experiencing of life as a series of conditions. Conditions, like the ability to double ourselves, are closed, circumscribed, static. Conditions are the limited horizons that our muted actions cannot transcend. One who dwells on conditions is a master of impressionistic analysis or, on the other end of the scale, a slave of circumstance who is powerless to act and to escape the condition by action. Indeed, "condition" (*Zustand*) is the concept we ascribe to actions because we wish not to account for the actions, *i.e.*, one ascribes a condition to a series of actions from which one tries to distance oneself, or which one no longer has the energy to apprehend or follow.

Hofmannsthal wrote, "There are countless things that for us are nothing but triumphal parades and pastoral plays of beauty . . . that we summon when our thoughts are not strong enough to find the beauty of life" (*Prosa I*, 157). The experience of life as a series of actions would not necessarily deprive life of beauty, insomuch as it would place us in life affirmatively, with the strength and presence to apprehend life and its "non-pastoral" beauty, to not only observe beauty Platonically, so to speak, but to engage in the experience of beauty.

As if to put to the test his metaphor of the chalice from the d'Annunzio essay, Hofmannsthal wrote one of his most popular poems, "The Two" ("Die Beiden"). The poem is widely anthologized and frequently held out as a model of Hofmannsthal's lyrical craftsmanship. "The Two" can be read aesthetically as romantic lyric poetry simply by accepting the beautiful images at face value. In the first strophe a girl bears a cup of wine to the rider; her features and her walk are so graceful that she approaches the rider, chalice in hand, with a smooth, fluid motion: "So light and certain was her gait, / That nothing from the chalice spilled" (*KA*, I, 50). The next strophe presents an image of the rider who is casual but firm in his control of the horse; the spirited horse is compelled to stand in a condition of trembling potential at the rider's command. So far the two beautiful images express only potential, insofar as the girl has not reached the

rider with her gift and the rider has not been able to accept it. Hofmannsthal deliberately destroys the imagery by introducing the third
and final strophe with "and yet"; upon nearing the completion of
their action the figures are unable to execute the stirrup cup without
spilling the wine: "For both of them they trembled so, / That no hand
found the other hand, / And dark wine rolled down to the ground."

The reader should not be lulled by the lyrical devices in the poem,
its complicated rhyme scheme (*a a b b, a b b a, a b c c a b*), vowel music, alliteration, and lapidary images; everything contributes to an
aesthetic crescendo whose point is decisively not aesthetic. The poem
should be considered in the light of the d'Annunzio essay, and the
metaphor of the brimming chalice that life holds out to us but that we
are unable to drink to the bottom because the chalice is cracked. As
readers of poetry we are inclined to read aesthetically, but a decon-
structed reading of "The Two" is closer in spirit to Hofmannsthal's
frame of mind.

The two figures are in themselves closed, without contact, as long
as the mediating stirrup cup is not drunk. However beautiful and
graceful and full of life she may be, and however skillful and brave
and masterful he may be, both of them remain apart as long as the all-
important action they have embarked upon remains undone. What
Hofmannsthal gives us in each case is a mood, or a condition, but no
action, and this he underscores by having the wine, which symbolizes the consummation of life, spill to the ground. Glamour, charm,
beauty, and elegance are no substitutes for the drink of life. The aesthetic reader is free to "interpret" the poem by exhausting himself in
the images, by lamenting the cruelty of the botched gesture, by perhaps speculating on the identities of the figures and attributing per-
sonae to them—but Hofmannsthal did not write the poem to capture
and frame a precious moment of Viennese *fin-de-siècle* languor. In his
essay "Poetry and Life" ("Poesie und Leben") from 1896 he claimed
that ever since the Vedas and the Bible "all poems can only be comprehended by lively persons, can only be enjoyed by the lively. A cut
stone, a beautiful weave always gives itself up, a poem perhaps once
in a lifetime" (*Prosa I*, 267). The German *lebendig* literally means
"lively," and "vivacious" hardly seems closer. The noun *Lebendigkeit*
means "liveliness," but capacity for life and appetite for living, and
not merely high spirits or hedonism, are included in that definition.
The emphasis on Hofmannsthal's *lebendig* is biological, as it is in
Goethe and Nietzsche.

Once again the question of paralysis of the will arises, because the poet himself, exercising his mediating but quasi-involuntary role as a leaking vessel, cannot *by his own volition* complete the action that mirrors life. The closest he can come is to embrace as much life as he can hold. If the poet "allows" his principals to consummate life in the poem, then life is not consummated in the listener or the reader: "all poems can only be enjoyed by the lively." Hofmannsthal infuses a maximum of life into the poem by not substituting his experience for ours. If Hofmannsthal had insisted on living the action for us, the poem would have "spoken" in the sense that Sartre insists the poem must not speak. As it stands, "The Two" is not silent.

An aesthetic reading of "The Two" poses serious problems in the context of meaning, as Benjamin Bennett has shown. In his interpretation the poem is "an allegory of verbal communication," and the conclusion, far from representing only a failure to link up, strikes a link on the reader's level "even though the contents of the goblet are spilled. For the content of the utterance, even though it is not successfully transmitted from the young lady to the young man, *is still there*, for all to see, in the poem's last line."[9] Bennett thoughtfully outlines the hermeneutic implications of the spilled wine, but does not make any attempt to situate the poem within the infrastructure of the chalice and its contents as seen from the vantage point of the philosophy of life. It remains clear, however, whether by my reading or Bennett's, that Hofmannsthal was concerned with the action of the spilled cup as the demonstrable, discernible sign to the living, a fact that Bennett underscores when he insists that poetry does not teach us about life through reading, but instead, "we understand poetry *by* living, by experiencing the abysses and pinnacles of the human condition."[10]

9. Bennett, *Hugo von Hofmannsthal*, 76, 78.
10. *Ibid.*, 28.

4 PREEXISTENCE

Paralysis of the will does not choke life to death, but it does distort it, bend it, and obstruct the flow, just as the cracked chalice allows life's promise to spill to the ground even as we try to drain the cup. We of course get enough to remain alive, in an offhand way, but according to Hofmannsthal we are not truly alive. His early short story "Fairy Tale of the 672nd Night" ("Märchen der 672. Nacht") is a case in point; the protagonist, as Richard Exner explains, "often feels that not only he himself, but also his life is observed from the outside."[1] The confusion and self-doubling that the merchant's son of "Fairy Tale" experiences define the limits of his existence—they are the consequence of not being able to break out of the condition of "unliving" that Hofmannsthal called preexistence (*Präexistenz*). A life that is consummated by actions, as opposed to being experienced as conditions, breaks out of preexistence, whereas a life that knows itself only as a condition tends to be dreamlike, and the unliving become detached, able to view their doubles. Hofmannsthal indicated in his *ad me ipsum* notes that viewing one's double is a sign (*Vorzeichen*) of "coming to oneself" (*KA*, I, 179).

But Hofmannsthal was apparently not fond of ontological speculation, so that his notion of preexistence can be construed more as a mystical, intuitive statement than a philosophical one. This he confessed to his father in a letter of August 13, 1895, pointing out that he should not look for profound or philosophical meaning in "Fairy Tale" (even though readers quite justifiably had this reaction).[2] Werner Metzler has also addressed this issue; the time span between birth and death does not necessarily correspond to Hofmannsthal's interpretation of existence, and occupying a bodily presence for a period of time

---

1. Richard Exner, *Hugo von Hofmannsthals "Lebenslied"* (Heidelberg, 1964), 56.
2. Hofmannsthal, *Erzählungen 1* in *KA*, XXVII, 208.

does not guarantee existence any more than merely being alive guarantees that a person has life in Hofmannsthal's sense of the word.[3]

The unliving exist, but at a different level, in a different state that can be described as preself. In "Experience" ("Erlebnis") the poet describes a condition of nebulous, descending darkness in which his thoughts grow dim "And silently I sank into the weaving / Transparent sea and departed this life" (*KA*, I, 31). Twilight-waking or twilight-sleeping provides the transition from life to a wondrous realm full of blossoms, colors, and music that is intuited as death: "That is death. It has become music, / Powerfully longing, sweet and darkly glowing." The poet has by this time departed life as he knew it, and emerged into a realm totally unfamiliar to him, though he intuits the realm as death.

Hofmannsthal separates the poem into halves by providing his own literal-textual transition; line 18 reads only "But how strange!" The narrative continues in first-person for two lines, then shifts to third-person. The narrator feels an acute nameless homesickness for life, such that his soul begins to weep soundlessly, but the rest of the experience is recounted from the narrator's point of view as he observes himself in childhood. The weeping of his soul, he explains, was like the crying of one who sails past his hometown on a great sailing ship, toward evening on the dark blue water.

> There he sees
> The streets, hears the fountains splashing, smells
> The fragrance of lilacs, sees himself,
> A child, standing on the shore, with child's eyes.

The ship keeps sailing, however, even though the narrator is able to see into his own eyes "that are fearful and want to cry." He can see light in his own room through the open window, but this closeness to himself cannot avail him since the ship continues to glide silently over the water "with yellow strangely billowed giant sails."

The mystical dimension of "Experience" is already suggested in the title; as dreamlike as the event may be, the poet chooses to refer to it as experience, as something that actually happened. Exactly what happens here remains a matter of interpretation, and on this point I have to agree with Michael Hamburger when he writes, "The degree of irrationality in a poem is one of its intrinsic and authentic qualities; it should be recognized and respected, not explained

3. Metzler, *Ursprung und Krise von Hofmannsthals Mystik*, 49.

away."[4] This is why I frame the "experience" of the poem with mysticism. The concept of preexistence is itself mystical, not ontological, but the poet Hofmannsthal has initiated the dialogue between himself and his reader, thereby inviting the reader, to the extent that empathy allows, into his experience according to the reader's own terms and frame of reference.

The unliving narrator has no time to enjoy the sweet melancholy of his death, since immediately he begins to sense a painful longing for life. The weeping of his soul is a response to the loss of life, which is described by the narrator in a detailed "as if" clause in which most of the senses are present; he sees the streets of his hometown, hears the fountains, smells the lilac blossoms, and most painful of all, sees into his own childhood eyes and senses the anguish in them. The narrator is on a voyage that takes him beyond death and beyond life, so that he is helpless to return to his own past to console the boy, but also helpless to return to his past life to be the boy that he was. That opportunity is lost, if one accepts the events of "Experience" as the historical fate of the narrator. But under any other circumstances, that is, accepting these events not as final but as an experience "like a dream" from which one returns to life, or to the unliving life of preexistence, the poem indeed captures that "coming to oneself" Hofmannsthal referred to in his notes.

Having experienced death as a condition of sweet melancholy, as "powerfully longing" music, the poet is suddenly overpowered by a longing for life. Death was not horrible, so that escape from death is not motivating. Death has no identifiable features, no town with familiar streets, only weird blossoms and jungles aflame with strange light. The longing for life, on the other hand, is a motivating factor for the experience of the poet's childhood self. Moreover, it is not entirely clear that the longing for life subsequent to the poet's death is a longing for the same life that he "departed" during the twilight state—it is more likely that now, having experienced what he thought was life, and having experienced death as well, the poet's longing is for the true, consummated life that he only intuits and glimpses, in passing, as he makes his approach to life, as he comes to himself. The childhood self symbolizes that life, and the poet-narrator of "Experience" is left with more than preexistence, but less than life.

In "Ballad of the Outer Life" the meaningless appearances of life changing to death evoked the question, "What good is all of this and

4. Hamburger, ed., Introduction to *Hofmannsthal*, xxxi.

these games, / To us who are big and eternally alone anyway?" (*KA*, I, 44). In notes to this poem Hofmannsthal placed an asterisk on the word "eternal" and explained, "in preexistence" (*KA*, I, 224). Pivotal here is the notion that in preexistence we do not have actual contact with society, we are isolated and exiled, just as the ship passenger of "Experience" is permitted to sail past his hometown community, even to sail past himself as a child, without being able to establish contact.

Preexistence, as Hofmannsthal wrote, is the "glorious but dangerous condition" (*KA*, I, 224) because from that state we have special powers of vision and understanding, without essentially having joined the living. Seen in this light, the uttering of the special word "evening" that marks the turning point of "Ballad" is another glimpse from the realm of preexistence to the higher, open life. Hamburger has described the prevailing condition of the poem as one in which "the identification of the man with the thing has broken down," with the result being an effect opposite of the Lord Chandos continuous intoxication: "Where the mediation of the dream is withdrawn, the things of this world are emptied of all meaning."[5]

Hofmannsthal carried the notion of preexistence as a form of exile, a lesser life, into the poem "Some of course . . ." ("Manche freilich . . ."). The first two strophes detail a seeming dichotomy between those who dwell below and those who dwell above. The poet explains that some must die belowdecks, "Where the heavy oars of ships are dipping," while others dwell above near the helm and have knowledge of birds in flight and the constellations (*KA*, I, 54). Some, he continues, lie with inert limbs among the roots of tangled life, while others occupy chairs among the sibyls and the queens, where they exemplify lightness of being.

The third strophe serves as a transition using Hofmannsthal's familiar "yet" (*doch, jedoch, dennoch,* etc.) to dispel the mood; a shadow, the poet explains, falls from the former lives into the others, so that "The light ones are bound to the heavy / As they are bound to air and earth." This transitional strophe marks not only the blending of lowly with elevated but also the shift in narrative perspective; from here the poet begins to use first-person:

> The weariness of long-forgotten peoples
> I cannot sunder from my eyelids,

5. *Ibid.*, xl–xli.

Nor distance from my startled soul
The mute descent of distant falling stars.

Many fates are weaving next to mine,
Existence plays them in and through each other,
And my lot is more than this life's
Slender flame or narrow lyre.

(*KA*, I, 54)

The poet first perceives of the out-there as a realm of division that is bridged by the shadow falling from one to the other, binding heavy and light; their separation exists only temporarily, or let us say, only on the individual, differentiated level, since on the whole they stand in relation to one another as air to earth. The individual poet, similarly, confesses that he cannot rid himself of the weariness of civilizations long since faded, extending his empathy temporally and collectively as well as to the falling stars that startle his soul despite the enormous distance and the fact that they are objects, not mortals. The poet maintains an intuition of his connectedness to all fates and all things, of the relative smallness of his individuation. This intuition occurs in a middle zone that lies between preexistence and selfhood.

"Secret of the World" also suggests the middle zone. The deep well preserves knowledge of the fact that at one time all were deep and silent and all shared this knowledge. With the advent of language, however, and the lapse of existence into babble that can only sustain poetry, song, and intuitions that momentarily cross over from the prelapsarian source to language-oriented, unconscious living, words constitute the middle zone that imprisons us just as the pebble imprisons the gem that is stepped on by the beggar. Hofmannsthal's notes to "Secret": "The ambivalent condition between preexistence and life. Coming-to-oneself (coming back to higher existence) by a direct route. This is a basic motif in 'Dream of Great Magic' and likewise 'the deep well surely knows'—wherein the deep well operates as one's own self" (*KA*, I, 219).

Hofmannsthal identifies the operation of coming to oneself as a coming back to higher existence, which in the context of "Secret" would mean transcending the word in order to return to deep, mute knowledge shared by all. This involves a paradox, however, since language is our means of approaching the source (higher existence) but language in its peculiar human restriction has us living a dream that twitches about in a circle ("Nun zuckt im Kreis ein Traum herum") (*KA*, I, 43).

There is hope for breaking out of preexistence into life and authentic selfhood, but as has already been discussed in the linguistic context of "Secret," this "coming up to what is proper, what is authentic [*aufs Eigentliche*]" cannot set in as dream or trance; it must set in "as proper fulfillment of destiny" (*KA*, I, 219).

The dream's relationship to preexistence is nowhere more evident than in "A Dream of Great Magic" ("Ein Traum von grosser Magie"). In the first and the final strophes of this poem of fifteen 3-line strophes the poet claims that he "found" the dream. This notion of "finding" the dream as opposed to dreaming it, as opposed to having it occur, implies a separation between subject and object. The poem begins in first-person, shifts to third-person in order to describe the activities of the great magician, then concludes in first-person after Hofmannsthal separates the last two strophes with a line of ellipsis points. The title's noncommittal "A Dream" also suggests that Hofmannsthal was trying to avoid associations connected with expressions such as "I dreamed" or "a dream came to me."

The events of the dream are centered around a great magician whose powers allow him to shape the earth and pull its depths to the surface: "He stooped and his fingers went / Into the ground as if it were water" (*KA*, I, 52). As the dream landscape changes, the great magician leaps atop a cliff: "—In him I saw the power of gravity end." The five strophes thus far devoted to the magician are concerned with his ability to penetrate solids, to rearrange the elements from solid, to water, and back to solid in the form of huge opals, and to easily defy gravity. In contrast to the giant leap taken by the magician in strophe 8, the next strophe begins to feature reflective operations. "In his eyes however was the peace / Of sleeping and yet lively precious stones" (*KA*, I, 53).

Hofmannsthal continues to detail the reflective operations of the magician. Still in strophe 9 he seats himself and speaks the word "You" as a pronoun of address, but the magician is addressing himself to days long since past. On the strength of this "You" he is able to summon those long-forgotten days ("daß sie herkamen") and this pleases him so much that he is moved to laughter and tears. At this point the poet's or the dreamer's empathy with the magician begins to sharpen, possibly as a result of the magician's intervention in the affairs of mortals (using the language of address, reviving the past). The dreamer sees that the magician laughs and cries, but senses that his reaction is one of joy upon successfully animating the past.

This empathy emerges strongly in strophe 11:

> He felt dreamlike the lot of all mortals
> Just as he felt his own limbs.
> To him nothing was near and far, nothing small and great.

Meanwhile as below him the night is falling, with the cooling of the earth and the darkness rising up from the depths,

> He savored all of life's great course
> So much, that in great drunkenness
> He bounded like a lion over crags.

The great magician turns his attention to the mortal sphere, so that days "that seem long gone to us" are resurrected, brought back to him. He is obviously just as capable of manipulating time as he is able to conquer space. The powerful empathy of the magician is demonstrated by Hofmannsthal through the dreamer's empathy with the magician; the fate of all humans becomes as familiar to the magician as the feeling he has for his own limbs—in his own limbs, *i.e.,* it becomes a part of him. The poet-dreamer must also experience this sensation in order to have sufficient empathy with the magician to share it. The magician has no concept of space and time, no notion of distance and proportion, because he is part of everything and everyone. When he sits down atop the cliff, his experiences are no longer directed at the phenomenal world, but instead toward the living world of humans, in which empathy plays a vital role. The magician becomes drunk with the course of life (*Gang:* course, progression, movement) such that his reflective, inward animation transforms to physical animation. We are given no indication of his direction or destination, we learn only that his intense savoring of life animates him to continue to defy gravity, to move on aggressively, like a lion. A being capable of pulling life into itself would respond just as the magician has responded, and discharging the accumulated surfeit of vitality is not a matter of choice, or a matter of goal or direction—it is simply a matter of discharging what must be discharged, releasing what has been accumulated. This reading of the magician's buoyant departure is in close accord with Nietzsche's will to power; life forms do not strive primarily to survive, but to appropriate and to discharge.[6]

The last strophes of "A Dream" represent a significant assessment as they return to first-person:

6. Nietzsche, *Werke,* II, 578, 728–29.

Cherub and high lord is our spirit,
Dwells not in us, and among the stars above
It sets its chair and leaves us orphaned much:

Yet He is fire in our deepest core
—This I sensed as I found the dream there—
And speaks to the fires of that distance

And lives in me as I live in my hand.

(*KA*, I, 53)

Man's spirit, or mind, or soul is represented in two ways: as a cherub signifying a lesser attendant of God, and as a mighty lord in its own right. When the poet insists that human spirit does not reside within us, but out in the stars, he could be referring to our ability to "find" such dreams as the one in question, where clearly factors greater than mere individuality are at work. "We" are left orphaned because we, individually and collectively, are not the possessors of spirit, only its occasional beneficiaries.

Hofmannsthal capitalizes the pronoun "He" in the final strophe, but not in the penultimate one, so that I attribute this pronoun to the great magician, and not necessarily to the human spirit (which is also masculine, *der Geist*). This convention in German usually denotes reference to God, the Lord, but the outcome of the poem doesn't change whether or not we regard "Him" as the great magician or God. It is conceivable that the great magician has been God all along, and equally conceivable that God never enters the picture. What is clear, however, is that the great magician sets in motion a dialogue with the human world by uttering the wondrous "You." This dialogue continues; while we remain orphaned by our own spirit, which seems to prefer a dwelling among the stars instead of a dwelling among mortals, where it would accomplish the most good, "He" serves as the fire in our innermost being. This juxtaposition between our roaming spirit and the great magician-animator is strengthened by the transition from penultimate to final strophe; following the colon is the qualifier "Yet," which has here the same strength as "however," "on the other hand."

Our deepest core is animated by his fire, and what's more, he "speaks to the fires of that distance." The distance referred to here is linked to the deepest core, which is a great distance from ourselves, perhaps as great as the distance from earth to the stars. He speaks to the fires that animate us and therefore he must possess more than a wraith existence, he cannot be a phantom or dream image; indeed, he "lives in me as I live in my hand." The great magician who is life, who is animation, had felt the fate of all mortals as clearly, as concretely, as he was able to feel his own limbs. Hofmannsthal transfers this analogy to the conclusion of his poem, insisting that the great magician is as real and vital to him as is his own hand. The connection between man and the higher existence that man must return to through the achievement of self is recognized in dream, dream in this case representing the portal or threshold between unliving and living. Our spirit wants to dwell elsewhere, and indeed it does dwell elsewhere during waking, preferring to leave us without spirit, without animation, without fire on earth. The one who establishes our potential to live is the great magician, life itself, capable of feeling total empathy with the fate of mortals and all of life; this great force will keep alive the fires that enable us to know the feeling of our own limbs.

A good deal of symbology could be applied to this poem, but I have tried to avoid it. The lion, the being springing from cliff to cliff, could be seen as Nietzschean fare, along with the magician's conquest of gravity and his being drunk on life. The great magician's relation to mortals is strikingly Promethean, as is his relation to fire. Explication of the symbols is generally interesting, but here it would detract from Hofmannsthal's effort to use a symbol to express a thing in its essence, not to substitute for it.

Dream is required to negotiate the approach or coming-up to higher self, but as Hofmannsthal distinguished in his notes, the higher existence is itself not a trance or a dream. The frequent allusions to *Ahnung* and its verb *ahnen* in Hofmannsthal's poetry, as well as the references to recollecting, point back to preexistence and are according to Hamburger "the processes that characterize" it.[7] *Ahnen* has always been a difficult term for translators, because there is no single corresponding verb in English that successfully links up the verb with its subject. The words that can be used are *anticipate, intuit, sense,* to have a *premonition* or *presentiment* of something, to have a *notion* of something; Webster's definition of *premonition* as an "anticipation of an event without conscious reason" seems to capture the meaning.

Ahnung plays a role in the poem "At times unloved women approach . . ." ("Zuweilen kommen niegeliebte Frauen"). In dream, the poet writes, the unloved women approach us as little girls and we are unspeakably stirred to behold them, "As if long ago on distant paths /

---

7. Hamburger, ed., Introduction to *Hofmannsthal*, xlii.

They walked with us at evening time" (*KA*, I, 46). The unloved or never-loved women (*niegeliebte Frauen*) embody a potential, a condition of anticipation or waiting, that Hofmannsthal extends also to the dream landscape that forms the rest of the poem. While the branches of the trees stir, the falling of night brings fragrance and a certain anxiousness (*Bangen*), and along their dark path "In evening glow the silent ponds glitter." The glittering of the ponds is a "mirror of our longing, twinkling dreamlike," and the souls of the walkers are described as sisterly, deeply trembling, and sad to all the night's effects, its soft words and its twinkling stars. But the souls are not only in empathy with the night, they are

> filled with triumphant splendor
> Of deep anticipation, that comprehends
> Great life and its grandeur and severity.

The poem therefore touches all three realms central to Hofmannsthal's poetics: dream as the threshold or catalyst for approaching life, preexistence as the source of heightened powers of intuition, and the great, open life that is comprehended by the intuition and in this poem appropriately serves as the destination, the dissolution of the evening walk.

In his notes Hofmannsthal revealed what parts are played by the various elements in the poem: "I Evening plain needs murmuring glittering water: II heart needs a woman: III love needs vague Platonic ideal dreams I II III are conditions encased within each other" (*KA*, I, 234). The unloved women who approach us ("kommen . . . uns entgegen") and are so capable of moving us fulfill the expectation of Part II; the poet transforms the unloved women through the medium of dream into little girls, but they are immediately transformed through the medium of recollection into partners from the past using the "as if" clause. The landscape needs glittering water, in this case the ponds that reflect the last glow of evening and then the light of stars, because without it there is no correspondence, no dialogue. The land would lie mute and still, virtually dead, if it were not reflecting light, as eyes that are dead no longer reflect. These same ponds not only provide light for the walkers, acting as beacons, perhaps, but also mirror their longing, once again pointing to interdependence. The longing of the evening strollers is animated, captured in the twinkling ponds.

The third condition to be satisfied is love's need for "vague, Platonic, ideal dreams." Hofmannsthal uses the expression "the souls" in the final strophe, bringing to mind the Platonic concept of soul. The souls feel empathy with all the night's events—they are in a sisterly relation to them and are filled with a vast, profound anticipation (or *sense*) of the great life, not the merely individual earthly life, but the life of Platonic dimensions that would correspond to the higher existence. Without its Platonic sublimation, love would exhaust itself in the here and now, in preexistence, or perhaps it would remain trapped in the middle zone. Without its Platonic sublimation and mode of egress, love would not be in a position to remedy the situation of the unloved women. These women would remain unloved, locked within the temporal-historical circumstances that contributed to their remaining unloved, and so the meaning of love would be reduced to the physical. It is precisely this limitation of love that Hofmannsthal denies.

The significance of *ahnen* for the poem "A Dream" can be demonstrated briefly by contrasting Hofmannsthal's use of the verb "to feel" (*fühlen*) with "to sense" (*ahnen*). In strophe 11, after the great magician has recalled or brought back long forgotten days, "He felt dreamlike the lot of all mortals" (*KA*, I, 53). The dreamer is able to sense that the magician *feels* this empathy because the magician has the greater powers, *i.e.*, the magician would not have to settle for "sensing" or "intuiting" the fate of humans since he actually feels it (though dream-like). By contrast, the dreamer speaking of his own experiences, using first-person in the final strophe, describes his understanding of the magician as the fire of our soul by saying "—This I sensed as I found the dream there—" (*KA*, I, 53). The dreamer is in this respect less real, less authentic, less alive than the animated core of his soul, namely, the great magician, but the life he possesses and feels in his own hand is indeed real, an understanding conveyed to him by his ability to sense or divine the magician's role. Hofmannsthal defines this difference between life and preexistence using words that illustrate the relative distance from life.

The joining with life that occurs when preexistence is stirred by the events of the middle zone is not without its darker side. From his study of Goethe and Nietzsche and from his own observations Hofmannsthal understood at a very early age that involvement in the great life, in higher existence, brings with it the baggage of guilt. This understanding animates "The Sin of Life," for example, and can be illustrated further by pursuing the thread of all-connectedness that runs through the poems.

All-unity, or all-connectedness, is a mystical concept that weaves the fate of mortals into the existence of all things. Hofmannsthal established a pattern of interjecting the dream into preexistence in order to summon the higher existence in which all things are connected. "We are such stuff as dreams are made on . . ." ("Wir sind aus solchem Zeug . . .") is perhaps the most succinct articulation of the phenomenon of joining with the world. The poet begins this *terza rima* poem by stating that we are made of the same substance as dreams, then he immediately personifies the dreams by likening them to little children who open their eyes beneath cherry trees just in time to see the full moon rising through the crowns of the trees: "Not otherwise do our dreams come out" (*KA*, I, 48).

The vivaciousness of children is transferred to dreams, "They are there and live like a child that laughs," and in the final strophe Hofmannsthal describes the working of dreams:

> The innermost is open to their weaving,
> Like spirit hands in a locked room
> They are in us and always have life.
>
> And three are one: a man, a thing, a dream.
> (*KA*, I, 48)

The unity of man and dream suggests that dreams are not mere images, figments of the imagination, but every bit as real as our livelier selves (children). The personification of dreams is very effective, for normally we regard dreams as detached, apart from us; dreams occur to us, intruding, sometimes menacing and sometimes seductive, frequently only confusing. Hofmannsthal evokes an empathy for dreams by giving them the receptiveness and capacity for living of the child, and this empathy flows back into "us" because *we* are the stuff of dreams.

Dreams operate uninhibitedly within us, their spirit hands are capable of weaving to the "innermost." In his translation of the poem Hamburger writes, "Our innermost life is open to their weaving."[8] I prefer to preserve Hofmannsthal's "the innermost" (*das Innerste*) without specifying that this innermost is us; lines 11 and 12 make it sufficiently clear that dreams are within us, working there, and capable of penetrating our "locked rooms." This innermost remains unspecified in the poem, and whereas I do not doubt that we, as mortals, are part

8. *Ibid.*, 31.

of the innermost, it seems to me that the innermost refers to all things and has the broad, encompassing connotations of things existing in their propriety. In other words, dreams penetrate to the core, dreams pull together mortal and thing, weaving themselves into the weave of the other. If dream animates or sets in motion the approaching of mortal and thing, then it is because dream is the proper medium for displaying and activating the powers of preexistence. Apprehending a thing in its essence, establishing its *proprium,* is the particular function of the symbol according to Hofmannsthal, and when dream weaves, or spins its yarn, or otherwise puts man in feeling contact with things, dream is performing a service analogous to the poet's work when the poet is at his best.

The short poem "Not at the sun's early journey . . ." ("Nicht zu der Sonne frühen Reise . . .") contains an emphatic underscoring of life's interconnectedness with dream. The entire poem of eight lines is a single sentence, progressing from time to manner as it attempts to suggest the connection:

> Not at the sun's early journey,
> Not when the evening clouds land,
> You children, neither loudly nor softly,
> Yes, hardly do we know ourselves
>   By which secret means
>   We wrested dream from life
>   And with grapevines gently
>   Bound it to our garden's fountain.
>
> (*KA,* I, 74)

The mystery of life's connection to dream occupies the poet in lines 1–5, but the conclusion deals with a certainty, albeit a certainty introduced "by secret means." The expressed certainties are embedded with implied certainties; "we," *i.e.,* we adults who might be expected to share some kind of understanding about life with our children, have employed secret means "to wrest dream from life." This wresting of dream from life implies a conflation or interweaving of the two such that, by whatever means, dream has to be extracted, separated, identified, and "cultivated" away from life, life being the great, indeed, the infinite expanse from which our dreams are culled. Our standing in life, our presence in the world, occurs mysteriously, yet we are the agents of this standing in life by virtue of further cultivating.

The image of the grapevine is used by Hofmannsthal in a manner reminiscent of Hölderlin's "Bread and Wine" and numerous other poems, but without the ontological clarity that Hölderlin tries to establish.[9] Wine and the abundant foliage of grapevines are symbols of Dionysus, who in turn symbolizes life through resurrection and abundance, through fertility and renewal. Hofmannsthal's contribution to the "wine equals life" nexus that was so richly explored by Hölderlin and Nietzsche lies in the extremely suggestive imagery of lines 6–8. After we manage, by unknown means, to harvest dream from life in such a way that we are able to sustain ourselves, *i.e.*, perceive of ourselves in the world as living beings, we are left not with a "piece of life" per se, but with dream. Dream is the medium through which we enjoy life—it is the measure of life that each of us gets.

In order for us to live the dream that is life, it becomes necessary to observe the link between dream and its source, life. For this purpose the vine is most appropriately suited; with the vine we "gently" bind the dream to the fountain of our garden, and the modifier "gently" is important here because it suggests an organic unity between dream and garden. The garden is what nourishes us, sustains us—it is indeed like the *notre jardin* of Voltaire's *il faut cultiver notre jardin.*[10] Our measure of life, given through dream, is the garden we must continue to cultivate. And this garden's fountain or well is in turn nourished by the dream-vine, its link to life. Our garden then is free to generate new life and to sustain our dream-life.

Written as the complement of "We walked" was "The Dominated One" ("Der Beherrschte"), which Hofmannsthal in his instructions to Stefan George, editor of *Blätter für die Kunst,* wished to have arranged in the journal immediately following "We walked" (*KA*, I, 330). Unlike "We walked," this poem's events take place within a dream. The dreamer is walking in the high mountains when

> Word reached me that they had found you
> And as my booty, with leafy tendrils
> They'd bound you to my garden tower.
> (*KA*, I, 75)

The images of binding with grapevines and tendrils carry over from "Not at the sun's early journey . . ." where these devices are used, by

9. See Del Caro, *Hölderlin,* in which I discuss wine, wine-making, wine as divine fire, and Dionysus as the bringer of the secret of wine-making.

10. See the conclusion of *Candide.*

secret means, to establish the living link between dream and life. It is therefore safe to assume that the "booty" of which the dreamer is notified is some personification of life, heretofore elusive but constantly sought after. The unspecified "they" are the dreamer's helpers, who seem to know that he desires this booty very much.

But here the title of the poem betrays its ambiguity. The "dominated" or "controlled" one had formerly been entitled "The Triumph" ("Der Sieg") (*KA*, I, 330), raising questions about who triumphs over whom, or what, and which is the dominated party. In his notes Hofmannsthal explained that not the booty is important to the dreamer, but the feeling of triumph (*Siegesgefühl*). This intense feeling causes the dreamer to have an inner sensation of being swept over immeasurable abysses, "as happens sometimes in looking at a small dark pond or when the cool air blows from empty spaces in the greenery" (*KA*, I, 331). This feeling of triumph in the dreamer suggests that he is the dominant one, for in this moment he has gained mastery over life such that his helpers are able to bind it to his garden tower.

But the dreamer as dominant one and life as booty hardly correspond to the mysterious, gentle, but thoroughly essential relations in "Not at the sun's early journey . . ." nor is this notion consistent with "We walked along a road . . ." ("Wir gingen einen Weg . . ."), where a reciprocity in giving and taking enables the heightened experience of life. The dreamer, now in control of himself, begins his journey homeward in the second strophe "with steady paces" ("mit gehaltenem Schritt"); at his side, like a flame, is "The reflection of your tousled hair / And your mouth, turned in anger" (*KA*, I, 75). If we are to take this personification to be the same one in the first strophe, then it is of course problematic for the booty to be accompanying him at one moment, in the mountains, flamelike at his side, while ostensibly it is bound to his garden tower somewhere down below.

But two things mitigate against this contradiction. First, it is the dreamer's sense of triumph, not the booty itself, that is operative in his dream experience; more "real" than the impossibility of restraining life in one's garden, by any means, is the sensation of triumph *as if* this were the case. And second, Hofmannsthal is not dealing with straight time in this poem. In dreams succession is not a rigid criterion, and even in life, as illustrated in "We walked," certain charged moments can contain such intensity that the barriers of the individual fall, allowing a gliding back and forth between small life and great life.

The dreamer concludes in the third strophe by claiming that he was proud,

> And striding calmly I perceived in the pond
> The play of a fish that seeks the dark,
> And above the wood the aerie of a vulture.
>
> (*KA*, I, 75)

Clearly the dreamer himself is the controlled one, and triumph describes the condition he enjoys upon triumphing over himself. However, the images of the final strophe should be considered in the light of Hofmannsthal's notes to this poem; the triumphant sensation, he explained, was like being swept or spirited over infinite abysses, borne aloft with the void gaping below, and this sensation was similar to the one experienced by looking at a darkening pond. This state is not one of domination or control, since the subject is under the sway of a far greater power than himself, capable of bearing him great distances over abysses.

Dominated by life in this sensation of triumph, the subject has to feel quickened, has to feel life extended beyond the ego. And yet, the dreamer claims: "But I was proud." The first-person recounting of the dream, and the frequent occurrence of "I" and possessive pronouns, are deceiving because they all point to the relation between subject, dreamer, and object—namely, his booty, life. But the triumphant feeling dissolves the subject and deconstructs the subject/object relationship, so that what remains in spite of the subject's lucid, controlled exercise of egocentric presence is the far greater presence of life, symbolized in the juxtaposition of the fish in the pond and the vulture in its aerie. Occupying their respective mediums, the playing fish and the vulture (*Geier*) reflect a reality in which terms like domination, control, and triumph are virtually irrelevant.

The unity of man, thing, and dream does not always demonstrate the innocence and receptivity of the child, nor is the weaving of dream in all cases "beautiful." Three years separate "We are such stuff . . ." and "The Young Man and the Spider" (Der Jüngling und die Spinne"), Hofmannsthal's revisitation of the concept of all-connectedness. The poem details the youth's encounter with two profound, poignant life events, the first connected mostly to himself, to his ego; the second, which represents a sobering and deeper understanding, is connected with the spider.

Hofmannsthal adds a dimension of drama to the poem by designating the youth as a dramatis persona and including stage instructions. Only the youth has lines, but the spider's role is given in the stage directions that intervene between the youth's initial intoxication and his new awareness. What motivates the youth, speaking "to himself with growing intoxication," is his feeling of triumph in love: "She loves me! How I now possess the world / Is beyond all words, all dreams" (*KA*, I, 70). His euphoria is nonetheless expressed in words that follow, and the youth is so pumped up by his elation that he threatens to break out of his principle of individuation:

> It is for me that from that dark peak
> The silent clouds drift in deeply lighted
> Space, seized by awesome dream:
> Thus it bears me—so that I do not waste myself!—
> To be the guest of living, sea, and land.

The inflated ego of the triumphant lover sees itself as the center of phenomena, and feels invited to sojourn everywhere, as the guest of life, etc. But on second thought, this status as mere guest is no longer sustaining to the youth, who revises his utterance. On the contrary, he maintains, only now does it dawn on him that he is not merely a guest in this world; the machinations of fate have demonically made him a master.

The youth envisions young boys who learn about life from him. Some of them resemble him, and he longs to see them grow up and come into their own; he senses "in a wondrous distant / Dream image my innermost unlocking / At the sight of what their deeds give me." The egocentric fantasizing culminates in a conflation of ego and world, ego and life:

> I am framed by the stuff of such
> Great life, to the great glow
> Of beautiful stars my drunkenness
> Is so closely related—
> For what future do I drunken one reach?
>
> (*KA*, I, 70)

The intoxicated youth attributes heightened powers of living to himself, and he believes, or feels, that *he* is instrumental in reaching for or awaiting some great future. The youth's ecstatic soliloquy concludes with a mystical "eternal feminine" tribute, at least insofar as he feels drawn upward, lifted to the stars and released from the earth. His future has already arrived, the moment is everything, and he feels himself invincible.

This raving is dispelled when the youth approaches the open window; Hofmannsthal uses stage directions to describe how the youth stands at the window that is illuminated by bright moonlight and framed by "the shadows of wild grape leaves" (*KA*, I, 71). Thus far the lover has been speechifying indoors, and his expansive, ebullient carrying-on is incommensurate with his location in the room, where he is cut off from the world. The open window invites him to look into the world, but Hofmannsthal signals immediately that the youth's glimpse into the world outside his window will not be a continuation of his ecstacy: The moonlight entering the room is "framed" by the shadows of grapevines, the latter serving as a reminder of greater life because they are the symbol of Dionysus.

From the darkness of one of these grape leaves a large spider creeps forth and pounces upon a smaller insect. The night is now so still that "an extremely soft, but pitiful sound" is heard, "and it seems one can hear the movements of violently choking limbs" (*KA*, I, 71). Upon viewing this tiny drama of terror, the youth is forced to step back and is seized by new emotions. Fear and distress cause his blood to ebb, his wonderful dreams become scattered, and the glorious fulfillment of his future, just moments ago charged with anticipation and destiny, "becomes empty and desolate." Already the youth has understood that his individuality, his ego, is not instrumental in the events of the world: "The world possesses itself, oh I am learning!"

The remainder of the lesson represents an affirmation of life on its own terms, as opposed to the egocentric, romanticized perceptions of the intoxication phase. The youth confesses that he does not hinder the disgusting spider's activity any more than he is instrumental in obstructing the orbit of stars, but what is more, he realizes that not only has he *observed* the phenomenon of life's violence, but "It takes place painfully within my heart." The violent spectacle unfolds within him, touching "every fiber" of his being, and he is resolute to walk this road without flinching, sensing as he does that such paths lead him homeward ("zur Heimat führen").

The youth now feels that he is impelled forward "with all his senses / Into uncertainty," and an incomprehensible, immense satisfaction settles over him in the form of anticipation (*Vorgefühl*):

> I will gain this:
> Suffering of pain, inflicting of pain.
> Now I shudder, sensing what surrounds me,
> It towers up to reach the highest stars,
> And now I know its name: its name is life.
>
> (*KA*, I, 71)

This "new life" is not viewed from the ego-center, so that the perspective includes not only unrestrained pleasure, but unmitigated suffering as well. Hofmannsthal was keenly aware of Nietzsche's philosophical conception of the Dionysian phenomenon among the ancient Greeks, so that he was always willing and able to counter the apparent "noble simplicity and quiet grandeur" of earlier conceptions of the Greeks with Nietzsche's reminder that life enjoins us to create beauty by virtue of having caused our suffering in the first place.

Hofmannsthal's *ad me ipsum* notes leave no doubt concerning his intentions in "The Young Man and the Spider." The need to break out of preexistence is experienced as a fear and a longing, the means for breaking out of it: "Connection to life. Penetration from preexistence into existence. The sweetness of incurring guilt, the pleasure of it, 'you lead us into life / you let the wretch become guilty / then you leave him to his pain' / W. Meister. . . . The sweetness of incurring guilt: because the connection to life is the penetration to being" (*KA*, I, 322). Illustrating his idea with Goethe's poem "Who Never Ate his Bread with Tears"[11] Hofmannsthal underscores how life demands the incurring of guilt and suffering of pain, and within the context of "The Sin of Life" I showed how Hofmannsthal, like Goethe, focused on the deed, on actions as experiences that anchor us in life and always leave a trail of "guilt" behind. But it was Nietzsche who provided Hofmannsthal with the climactic twist that in "The Young Man" results in a premonition of suffering that he will inflict on others.

Hofmannsthal had made note of aphorism number 325 from Nietzsche's *The Gay Science* as early as 1891 (*KA*, I, 323); "The Young Man and the Spider" was written in 1897. A line or two from the aphorism entitled "What Belongs to Greatness" is appropriate here: "Being able to suffer is the least part, weak women and even slaves become masters of this. But not perishing of inner distress and insecurity when one has inflicted great suffering and hears the cry of this suffering—that is great, that belongs to greatness."[12] Inflicting pain and causing suffering is not, in Nietzsche's view, a singularly human operation but a dimension of life that we choose to deny. If the youth is ever to abandon the shadowy realm of preexistence, then he must cross the threshold into living, where guilt is a factor. Hofmannsthal wrote of the "sweetness" of incurring guilt because guilt pulls us into

11. Johann Wolfgang von Goethe, *Wilhelm Meisters Lehrjahre*, in *Hamburger Ausgabe*, VII, 136 ("Lied des Harfners").
12. Nietzsche, *Werke*, II, 188.

life and represents a "penetration to being." This penetration to being, in turn, represents totality, completeness, so that despite its appearance the disgusting spectacle of exploitation, performed by the spider, serves to alert the youth to possibilities that are anchored in the world, not in the effusiveness of his ravings.

Very much in the spirit of Nietzsche, Hofmannsthal deconstructs a major Western ideal, namely, love, by demonstrating that it is not synonymous with life. And also in keeping with Nietzsche's campaign against idealism and romanticism, Hofmannsthal understood that ideals, like rampant language and marauding words, obstruct life and put it at a safe distance from ourselves. Living within ideals, even claiming to savor life and to be the favorite child of life, as in the case of the eloquent youth, is to live a charmed life. By charmed I mean here inauthentic, idealized to the point where egocentricism is the only standard for living. Like the youth's room, his idealization of love contained him, prevented him from connecting with the world outside his window. At the moment when the youth might have looked upon the moonlit night as just another extension of his ego, just another prize for his feverish longing, Hofmannsthal exploded the myth by having life manifest itself at the threshold. At first the youth is repulsed by what he sees: "You hideous force, you animal, you death!" (*KA,* I, 71), but soon the symbolic inoculation of the spider has penetrated every fiber of his being, so that the youth no longer indulges in perceptions of himself as privileged—he has learned his kinship with the spider.

5 THRESHOLD

Hofmannsthal's poetry is animated by the presence of threshold, movement, and crossing over. Poets frequently enjoy their success in capturing mood—in framing or freezing phenomena so that the reader is invited to dwell within a lyrical photograph—and we have come to expect this from a medium that deals in symbols and images. But Hofmannsthal was not content to deal in this medium along lines established by his predecessors, as conservative as his lyric poetry undoubtedly remains in other respects (use of rhyme, traditional verse, meter, etc.). As the language of life, to the extent that life speaks and the poet is able to serve humanity as the articulator of life, Hofmannsthal's poetry respects the fact that life is not static.

Here I wish to address the observations of Benjamin Bennett, who, concerned with "the inadequacy of the idea of a 'language of life,'" argues as follows: Just as Hofmannsthal rejects the possibility of actually transcending self-consciousness, so too is his poetic based "on a refusal to be deluded about the possibility of transcending conceptual language, or transcending language as writing. There is no transcendence."[1] Bennett's point is well taken, and what I have to defend is not a position contrary to his own but, instead, the manner in which I conceive of the "language of life."

Bearing in mind that my understanding of the philosophy of life is based on Nietzsche, and further bearing in mind that Nietzsche (as Bennett correctly recognizes) clearly informed Hofmannsthal's views on life, the phrase "language of life" contains certain qualifiers from the outset. The language of life is *that speech by virtue of which we are not casting about for a transcendental*. The language of life does not transcend experience (life), it apprehends life to the extent that the biological phenomenon "human" is able to articulate his presence in the

1. Bennett, *Hugo von Hofmannsthal*, 24.

world. It is my conviction that the poet is qualified to speak on this issue, not necessarily in the philosophical context of a Nietzsche, but by virtue of not having to lug or throw off the philosophical baggage that comes with philosophical breakthrough à la Nietzsche. Bennett is right in holding to the tenet that "there is no transcendence," for this truism applies to Nietzsche and Hofmannsthal equally. However, merely because there is no transcendence does not imply "there is no language," there is no poetry, there is no poetry capable of approaching life.

On one level I can sympathize with Bennett's aversion to the notion of a language of life, but it seems almost to parallel his aversion to "experiencing death," and these are not the same.[2] Nietzsche's critique of idealism, metaphysics, and the entire Platonic notion of transcendence resulted in a use of language that has contributed extensively to contemporary critical debate; Nietzsche liberated philosophy from itself, and imposed his own philosophizing via a language that strives to preserve the animation, tensions, and contradictions of life. It is in this spirit that Hofmannsthal and subsequent generations strove to animate language by linking it to life. Where language engages the problem of manifesting life, and especially where it succeeds in doing so, there is a language of life.

It is also a reflection of the times that Hofmannsthal was sensitive to movement and transition, since writers in the 1890s had the legacy of the nineteenth century to come to terms with, and in the case of Germany and Austria, many writers felt especially constrained by the goals and aspirations of the new Reich.[3] The greatest single figure to impart movement into the spirit of the 1890s was Nietzsche, quite understandably, because he made it his personal philosophical campaign to burn all bridges lying between himself and tradition, between himself in his role as the philosopher of life and the powerful romantic movement, which for him roughly began with Rousseau and culminated in Richard Wagner.[4] Seen historically, Nietzsche is the pivotal figure of transition from nineteenth- to twentieth-century thought, and young Hofmannsthal, as Bruno Hillebrand has perceptively observed, was the most outstanding figure of his generation

2. *Ibid.*
3. Hillebrand, *Nietzsche*, 2, 5.
4. See Adrian Del Caro, *Nietzsche contra Nietzsche: Creativity and the Anti-Romantic* (Baton Rouge, 1989), in which I systematically treat Nietzsche's understanding of romanticism and his relation to that movement.

when it came to coming to terms with Nietzsche before the turn of the century.[5]

Receptivity is a mark of anticipation. Those who are passively statal, merely persisting in stasis with respect to the world, do not exhibit the receptivity that is required for movement to take place, hence such persons would not necessarily recognize the open if it lay before them. It is also true that persons occupying a condition of stasis would not be motivated to *explore* the open—say, in the fruitful, truly enterprising spirit of the German romantics after Kant. Hofmannsthal frequently explored the open by experiencing, and detailing the experience of heightened states of receptivity.

The poem "Experience" begins with the description of a transitional state:

> With silver-gray hazes the valley
> Of twilight was filled, as when the moon
> Sickles through clouds. Yet it was not night.
> (*KA*, I, 31)

The premature or extraordinary twilight resembles night, but since it is not in fact night, it signals the presence of a heightened state. The poet next reveals that his dimming thoughts ("meine dämmernden Gedanken") begin to dissolve, so that he sinks within "a weaving / Transparent sea and departed this life." Hamburger translates *Duft* and *Dufte* literally as "fragrance," instead of poetically as "haze." I prefer to use "haze" because the poet is still in visual, cognitive contact with the world in lines 1–4, before he begins to depart this state in the rest of the poem. Hamburger's translation is good in suggesting synesthesia, another heightened state, here intimating that the poet sees fragrance.[6] The noun *Dämmerung* means "twilight" or "dawn," and its verb *dämmern* can likewise connote fading or growing light. The poet's experience is set off by the dimming of his thoughts, in my reading, because cognition is not capable of presenting him with the "experience" of death that lies in store, and his thoughts are said to have dissolved (*verschwammen*) because the *principium individuationis* at this point dissolves. From his twilight state the poet goes on to explore the open—traversing death, homesickness for life in death, the observation of his childhood double—and of course, upon emerging from the poem as from the experience, returns to the living in a changed state of mind.

5. Hillebrand, *Nietzsche*, 25.
6. Hamburger, ed., *Hofmannsthal*, 3.

Hofmannsthal alluded to a similar receptivity for transition in "Prologue and Epilogue." The poet is reciting his invitation to the viewers of the living paintings, urging them to leave behind their notions of beauty and artistic experience in favor of experiencing the "tiny art" that does not seize spectators. He enjoins them:

> Come all of you, and think yourselves alone,
> Alone in dimming and silent rooms . . .
> What things one imagines when one nods off
> With half closed eyes and sits in the evening
> Not fully waking, neither fully sleeping and dreaming!
>
> (KA, I, 38)

Hofmannsthal favors the twilight state because it offers freedom of perception:

> Thus images come, images go, dissolve,
> And everything is familiar and strange and charming;
> Not fully waking, and not fully a dream.
>
> (KA, I, 39)

What the poet does not promise the viewers of the event is a rational interpretation or sequence; there is not supposed to be a closure, so that images dissolve and the familiar and the strange are on equal terms. Through such receptivity the poet hopes to enable the *proprium* of the images to emerge; their lives (these are individuals depicting figures in paintings) as works of art are to be encountered, respected, just as we respect one another's lives.

The receptivity of "Experience" and "Prologue and Epilogue" begins with interiority and enables the subject to explore outer realms. Having abandoned cognition and the principle of individuation, the subject of "Experience" goes into death and into his past life, never leaving life. Having primed his fellow viewers for the experience of art by suggesting a twilight state in which cognition is not enslaving, the poet in "Prologue and Epilogue" essentially invites the guests to embark upon a journey in search of the "tiny art." The interiority of the guests or viewers will be dissolved so that they, as living beings, can enter into the open (here: art), just as the individuals who depict figures from the paintings can liberate themselves from the interiority of the plastic medium to join the open and become animate.

In other poems Hofmannsthal uses the landscape and the subject's relation to it to make a shortcut from stasis to transition, as for example in "We walked." One of the companions points to a mountain shrouded in shadows of the clouds and the other peaks, and says: " 'If only we two were there alone!'" (*KA*, I, 76). These words have an immediate and profound effect on the subject. They sound as foreign and exotic as sandalwood and myrrh, and even the companion's eyes do not seem as usual:

> And it happened that a drunken air
> Seized me, as when the earth quakes
> And toppled stately ornaments
> Roll around and water gushes from the ground
> And one stands reeling and sees double:
> For I was here and yet was also there
> With you, arm in arm and all the joy
> Of it was somehow mixed with all the joy
> That this great mountain with its many gorges
> Bestows if someone silently, like an eagle,
> Flew around it on outstretched wings.
>
> (*KA*, I, 76)

The subject experiences not only the heightened joy of being in two places at once—namely, the place of origin and the place of desire, the "wished for" place—but also the mountain's secret joy, with the special intimacy that only a soaring eagle could command, since the eagle and the mountain share great height. The companion's words have fallen on a receptive moment; the walkers are going along a road "with many bridges," so it is safe to infer that transitions are taking place frequently as gorges are crossed and they penetrate deeper and deeper into the mountain's heart.

The idea suggested by the companion is of course merely a wish, but under these circumstances, insofar as the two are obviously "high" in every sense of the word, the words are transformed and a threshold is crossed. The reality of not being in two places at once is challenged by the exotic-sounding wish; the subject associates the sound of the words with the fragrance of sandalwood, an implied synesthesia that alerts us to the point of transition. When the subject is seized by a drunken air ("eine trunkne Luft") it is as though he were being literally inspired by it.

There are stages or degrees of crossing over connected with the poem "We walked." The companions are crossing bridges along their way, but they are also taking in the scenery, and simultaneously being taken in by it. "Taking in" here is meant as absorption or admittance; the companion, in taking in and not merely viewing the landscape, *is taken into* the physical properties of the land in such a manner that a powerful diffusion of emotion erupts—the first "quake" of the poem—and the wish is uttered. By virtue of the activity the two are engaged in, namely, the physicality of both their *striding* and *taking in*, what might otherwise have been a mere walk in the mountains becomes an experience of the life that encompasses everything.

The higher degree of merging is undertaken by the subject who feels a drunken breath seize him, indicating that what transpires in the soul of the companion is overwhelming enough, in the sense of being able to overwhelm individuality, to touch them both. The liberating properties of physical activity cannot be underestimated here: It is well known that Nietzsche, favoring the mountain terrain of northern Italy, frequently made jottings in his notebook while he walked. In notes on this particular poem, Hofmannsthal wrote: "Encounter: I climbed down a slope among shrubs and thought how beautiful it is to give oneself and to possess—correlative concepts" (*KA*, I, 333).[7] The activity of climbing down a brushy slope suggested to Hofmannsthal the beauty of giving oneself and of possessing, *i.e.*, taking into oneself, and this operation is also reflected in the poem.

The giving and taking centers around the question, What do the mountains have to give? The walkers have already given themselves to the mountains, and this is how the mountains are able to respond. If the mountain that lies so secretively under shadow were merely viewed, or studied aesthetically, the walkers could not experience the "quaking" of the earth that initiates the subject into the experience of joy on two levels: The first joy involves the thrill of being in two places simultaneously, the second joy involves the thrill of empathy with the mountain and its lonely, isolated existence. The mountain represents the open, and it is only out in the open that such experiences can take place. "Out in the open" here refers to the life that encompasses all things, *i.e.*, the open that lies beyond the threshold of the everyday.

Normally the mountain would have no history, no life, no secret to convey because the subject, enclosed within the principle of individuation, would merely regard it as an object. Having experienced such a taking in and being taken in, it is no wonder that Hofmannsthal concluded the poem with an almost titanic feeling of kinship with the ancient gods, and referred to the walk in the mountains as "an adventure" (*KA*, I, 77). After all, the mountain with all its untrodden paths,

---

7. I cannot duplicate the orthography and arrangement of the note text as the editors have tried to do, but my arrangement and translation are as literal as possible.

deep gorges, and otherwise unassailable height "bestows" itself (*hingiebt*) to the subject as if he, the subject, were an eagle capable of circumscribing the mountain's vastness in flight.

A certain precariousness attaches to the experience of the threshold, such that a bridge or crossing over may sometimes result in less than ecstatic intuition. The openness of preexistence, magic though it is and capable of luring one into dwelling on the threshold, must be surpassed in the spiritually mature individual. Beyond the threshold lies life itself—"existence"—with its guilt, pain, and eternal contradictions. Hofmannsthal had a perfect opportunity to illustrate this idea in the experience that led to the poem "Travel Song" ("Reiselied"). This poem of only ten lines has several literary precedents, among them poems by Goethe, Eichendorff, and Brentano, because of the favored romantic theme of travel and the time-honored metaphor of life as journey (*KA*, I, 353).

In August of 1898, Hofmannsthal crossed the Simplon pass on a bicycle journey. The experience was even more impressive than crossing the Brenner, as he related in a letter to his father, and it was made so in part by the dark clouds that gathered on his ascent and the darkness and rain that came down as he approached the top (*KA*, I, 353). "Travel Song" is not, however, the kind of text that one would ascribe to romanticism. The first strophe of traditional cross rhyme is marked by the overpowering actions of nature: water cascades "to swallow us"; boulders roll "to crush us"; and on powerful wings birds come to bear us away (*KA*, I, 84). These perceptions are visually located at a high elevation, where the poet is able to gaze straight out and straight up. He is not the peer of the cataracts and glaciers and soaring eagles, but he has invaded their territory and harvested the sense of danger connected with dwelling on this side of the threshold. Here he is puny, unprotected, and in every respect *exposed* to the power of the open.

The two remaining strophes of three lines seem to liberate the stranded traveler from his dangerous isolation. "But," writes the poet, below there lies a land whose fruits are mirrored endlessly in ageless lakes; marble brow and fountain's rim rise from the blossoming landscape, "And gentle breezes blow." The poet's gaze is no longer a factor, having dissolved into an "inner" romantic gaze that speaks the language of earth as home, earth as garden. Hofmannsthal deliberately avoids any transition beyond the word "but" introducing the second strophe. Two worlds are evident here, and though one can be said to be a part of the other, different languages are at work.

Near at the top of the pass, as the storm gathers and darkness falls, the poet feels exposed and vulnerable. He speaks here for his community by using the pronoun "us." *We* are exposed to the powers of nature in existence; there is immediacy, there is also advocacy in the sense that the poet speaks for humanity at this level. The absence of pronouns in the poem's second part, and the abundance of romantic imagery, suggest the prethreshold stage of preexistence. The collective home or *Heimat* of romantic orientation is very much like the gentle, giving and forgiving landscape reflected in timeless quiet lakes. One knows that one can always return there mentally or spiritually, and its physical attributes are identifiable by means of the poetic maps left behind by the poets. Hofmannsthal has left the romantic landscape below him, but his experience of the summit is only temporary, and like the rest of humanity, he must return to hospitable regions.

Once the high pass is crossed and one is safely on the other side, an insight always remains in the individual. Existence carries with it the trace of the preexistent world. "We" are subjected to destructive, disruptive forces at the top, once we have transcended the lush harmony of romantic nature. In the letter to his father, Hofmannsthal described how clouds gathered and rain and darkness fell as he approached the summit of Simplon, so that if we transfer this timing to the poem, the switch from nonromantic to romantic or from conscious to unconscious would take place without visual contact. About the time Hofmannsthal reached the summit, "home" was no longer visible. He had trained his eye on the cataracts and glaciers, but suddenly they along with everything else are no longer visible. I am reminded again of Zarathustra's definition of seeing: "Is seeing not itself seeing into the abyss?"[8]

But Nietzsche's existential seeing cannot and must not be sustained too long. The courageous gazing upon abysses that quickens Zarathustra and temporarily occupies the poet must yield to a gentler language with a more hospitable open. Sojourning in the open without a way back to the familiar is spiritual suicide, while eschewing the open in favor of dwelling only in the familiar is preexistence, the unliving state. As long as the poet's eyes are trained on the glaciers and cataracts, "we" as a metaphor for humanity are entirely at the mercy of nature. As the physical darkness and the storm descend upon him, Hofmannsthal remains aware of the threatening surroundings but ef-

8. Nietzsche, *Werke*, II, 407.

fectively shields himself by summoning images of the friendly land. In this sense, perhaps, the romantically evocative term *Reiselied* is like a song celebrating travel or consoling the traveler whose existence takes him into hostile regions of the spirit.

Hofmannsthal spent two weeks in Lugano toward the end of summer in 1898, and his farewell to this unusually charming city, also the favorite of Hermann Hesse, addresses the theme of giving and taking as a threshold experience. Hofmannsthal's poem was finally entitled "From Aboard Ship" ("Vom Schiffe aus"), but his notes reveal an earlier title, "The Departing One" ("Der Scheidende"); both titles suggest the moving and moving on that is characteristic of the heightened receptivity necessary for crossing thresholds. "From Aboard Ship" refers to the steamer that Hofmannsthal boarded to cross Lake Lugano (*KA*, I, 367–68). The device Hofmannsthal uses to express his intimacy with the place is personification; the first three strophes address morning, noon, and evening with the pronoun "you" (*KA*, I, 88). Morning touched his bed with the special light of mussel-shell clouds and illuminated a distant path into the mountains that he was never able to locate later on ("den ich später niemals fand"). The earliest hours and their special radiance are a time of transition because they point the way to a distant path that the poet apparently attempts to walk but is unable to locate. The dispersing of night's darkness is bright and colorful, and the poet allegorically embarks on life and life's travels at this promising stage.

More penetrating is the light of the noon hour, that transitional hour specified by Nietzsche as the precise moment when man will make his transition to overman because there are no shadows for concealment. Hofmannsthal, however, describes a twilight state beneath a great dark tree,

> Where shallow waking and a shallow sleep
> Stole myself from me, that to my ear
> The hidden breath of gods reached not!
>   (*KA*, I, 88)

Nietzsche used the motif of the high or perfect noon throughout *Zarathustra* and even had Zarathustra experience a loss of self similar to the state described here by Hofmannsthal. In poetic terms the sun's brilliance at noon will drive us into the shade, inducing indolence and slumber while the gods are about.[9] This twilight slumbering deprives

---

9. *Ibid.*, 411–14, 512; I, 996–97.

the poet of self and therefore deprives him of powers of observation; unlike the fertile twilight state of "Prologue and Epilogue," this one suggests a lapse of self into oblivion. Continued in this strophe is the idea of not attaining a desired end, of not breaking through and crossing over.

The poet addresses himself next to the evenings, revealing that he turned

> from the shore
> Seeking conversations, and shoulders did not
> Ascend dripping from the deep, and my breath
> Dissipated in strife with shadows and with light.
>
> (*KA*, I, 88)

Once again, the poet's efforts to effect the transition, to establish himself in the open in dialogue with others, with the gods, perhaps, remain fruitless. His breath dissipates or "dies out" like a sound that fades (*verklang*) as it struggles with dark and light, competing futilely. The synesthesia here is not at all suggestive of heightened receptivity, but of its contrary; the poet is not at one with this world, but at two with it.

The fourth and final strophe deals no longer with the stages of day, and to underscore this separation Hofmannsthal concluded the third strophe with a colon:

> He now departs, who from the hand of life
> Here received no pain and no happiness:
> And leaves here also, for he cannot otherwise,
> A part of his soul behind.
>
> (*KA*, I, 88)

The first-person narrative of strophes 1–3 is replaced by a detached third-person. The early strophes are given a confessional aspect because the poet personifies and addresses the mornings, noons, and evenings spent in Lugano, and in so doing, these strophes take on a tone of lament. The conclusion is not clearly a lament, however, and its tone is one of taking stock, of weighing the balance.

The Lugano sojourn was not entirely a happy one for the poet, as he revealed to his parents in a letter of August 23, 1898, and Hofmannsthal confessed that despite the beauty of his surroundings he felt depressed (*KA*, I, 358). However, by August 30 he was able to inform them that he was "very satisfied" (*KA*, I, 368). The conclusion of "From Aboard Ship" reflects this restoration of balance to his spirit, with its understanding of the give-and-take that does not always favor us and shower us with blessings, as was the case in "We walked." The last two lines are particularly illustrative of Hofmannsthal's affirmation of life even when it did not lie open to him. He leaves a part of his own soul behind, in this place that was not giving, because "he cannot do otherwise." But far from leaving part of himself behind out of mere compulsion, the poet has recognized that things must be so, that it is in the nature of things to work sometimes in this way. I read the final line to mean the poet is not going to be petulant or stingy vis-à-vis the place of his sojourn; instead, in his understanding that the hand of life is not there for him alone, not always giving, he must leave a part of himself behind. It is this act of departing and leaving part of oneself behind that, effectively, marks a transition and contributes to the state of being open—others who sojourn in Lugano will conceivably experience a part of Hofmannsthal that remains there forever, just as we, his readers, have not been denied admittance to that open.

The crossing of a threshold to the open can be a mark of joining with greater life, but it has also been shown that sometimes the transition is achieved lethargically, retroactively, as in "From Aboard Ship" where the poet's receptivity seemed numbed. It is also the case that crossing the threshold establishes contact with death; to a limited degree this idea is present in "Experience," but I see in the conclusion of that poem a deep understanding of how the poet must maintain, cultivate the open *so that* he is not forever aboard the ship that passes him by. The life/death threshold was given a puzzling treatment by Hofmannsthal in his poem "Psyche," which bears the motto "Psyche, my Soul. Edgar Poe" (*KA*, I, 32).

The "psyche" of this poem has something in common with Poe's Psyche from his poem "Ulalume."[10] Like Poe's Psyche, Hofmannsthal's is also somewhat distraught and in need of comfort. Another feature in common is the poet's use of eloquence, word magic, to dispel Psyche's gloom. When Psyche mistrusts the star, she begs in terror to flee and finally collapses,

> letting sink her
> Plumes till they trailed in the dust—
> Till they sorrowfully trailed in the dust.[11]

---

10. See the editor's notes in *KA*, I, 181, 189, for possible sources in Poe, Moréas, and Nietzsche.

11. Edgar Allan Poe, "Ulalume—A Ballad" in Poe, *Selected Prose, Poetry, and Eureka*, ed. W. H. Auden (San Francisco, 1950), 476, 477.

The poet is able to console her by claiming they are only dreaming; he goes on to describe this dreaming in extremely hopeful terms, of course. The light of the star detested by Psyche is transformed by the poet into light "That cannot but guide us aright, / Since it flickers up to Heaven through the night." Psyche is then "tempted" out of her gloom and continues the journey that does, in fact, end in death at the vault of Ulalume.

A major difference is apparent in Hofmannsthal's psyche, for unlike Psyche, she is weary of life at the outset and expresses a desire for death. The poem begins:

> and psyche, my soul, looked at me
> pale and trembling from tears suppressed
> and said softly: "Lord, I wish to die,
> I am weary to death and I am cold."
>
> (*KA*, I, 32)

Hofmannsthal's poem is devoted next to "tempting" his soul with a potion: "Be still, I will prepare for you a drink / With good warm wine I will give you to drink." What follows is a lush, bright, and extremely dense portrayal of the "effervescent juice of vitality" and its properties. Hofmannsthal conjures up images of laughter, drunkenness, music and dancing, mirth, sunshine, blossoms and vines, pale women and luminous images, exotic lands and glowing clouds, beds of roses and hot gemstones.

But Hofmannsthal's psyche is not successfully tempted by this luscious feast:

> And psyche, my soul, looked at me
> And said sadly: "All these things
> Are dull and dreary and dead. Life has
> No lustre and fragrance. I am weary of it, Lord."
>
> (*KA*, I, 32)

It is at this point that the poet knows no other way to tempt psyche than to initiate her into the opposite realm, namely, death. He confesses: "I said: 'I know of yet another world, / If the living one does not please you.'" Psyche's troubles are apparently so deeply rooted that she does not respond to the inoculation of life proposed by the poet. Searching for a strategy that might exert a sufficiently potent remedy, he tries to liberate psyche from her gloom by unlocking the portals of dream.

Before he begins to persuade his soul, the poet this time expressly summons the power of words: "With wondrous words heard never before / I will throw open for you the portal of dreams" (*KA*, I, 33). Previously psyche was to have been consoled with a potion of life, so that the poet trusted life to work its magic on psyche. The bright, airy images of the daytime wooing of psyche therefore represent the least interference and distortion from language, whereas now, having arrived at his wit's end, the poet relies on "words heard never before" ("nievernommenen Worten") as if this magic were more powerful than life itself. The portal that he promises to throw open to psyche is the threshold from life, which is abundant in him, at least, to dream, and he uses the expression of throwing open the portal in line 30 and again in line 44.

The dream world that is revealed to psyche is a realm of darkness and confusion, in which the nocturnal, dark, and shadowy effects stifle the living and weave a spell of gravity upon them. Synesthesia is used to connote disproportion; there is the "fragrant dancing of laughing women," and the glowing of the sea is described as the rippling, greenish, drunkenly dancing, dark, sultry, and darkly gleaming digging of violins. As in the writing devoted to the daytime's living promise, but to a greater degree in this second part of the poem, Hofmannsthal uses profuse assonance, alliteration, internal rhyme, and end rhyme with images piling up and colliding. This technique fulfills the promise to use "words heard never before." The sea is further described "With bounding, resounding and searing and leering / Waves like the glinting of rivers of metal." Here is

> The homeland of winds, wailing wild in the night
> With shadows eclipsing the lakes of their light;
> And the land of metal, that in silence displays
> Its smolder 'neath heavens of iron and gray.—
> (*KA*, I, 33)

This realm beyond the portals of dream corresponds with Poe's:

> Well I know, now, this dim lake of Auber—
>   This misty mid region of Weir—
> Well I know, now, this dank tarn of Auber,
>   This ghoul-haunted woodland of Weir.[12]

Hofmannsthal suggested before he opened the dream portal that he would present psyche with "another world" if she could not be swayed by the living one, and certainly a land of smoldering metal lying beneath a sky of iron gray is not conducive to living.

12. *Ibid.*, 477.

The poem originally ended on this grim note. A soul that is weary of life, whose receptivity is at such a low that life's potion remains ineffective, should be given an opportunity to glimpse the other side, the alternative. The reader does not learn about psyche's response and the poet's fate. A year later, however, Hofmannsthal wrote a conclusion to the poem, but he remained as coy about the conclusion as his psyche remained about embracing life. Instead of appending the conclusion to the poem itself, he included it in his 1896 essay on d'Annunzio and attributed the lines to someone else (*KA*, I, 182). In denying authorship of the lines, he seems to have preferred the ending originally published, but in publishing the lines at all, albeit in a most roundabout way, he seems to have wanted the poem otherwise.

The conclusion is now included in the text of the poem, but it sheds only a weak light and offers almost nothing by way of closure. Then again, *it is not closure that the experience of the threshold offers,* but the open:

> Then psyche my soul looked at me
> With angry eye and hardened mouth and spoke:
> "Then I must die, if you thus know nothing
> Of all the things that life wants."
>
> (*KA*, I, 33)

On two occasions the poet attempted to lure psyche back into life affirmation. Her first insistence that life had no lustre or fragrance, and that the poet's best efforts to let life animate her were things "dull and dreary and dead," reveal that psyche's condition was beyond immediate repair. The best life could do, it seems, was not enough to persuade her that life is anything but dead, so she might as well be dead, too.

On the second occasion the poet once removed, *i.e.,* the poet making a conscious effort to breach psyche's neurosis by virtue of his extraordinary gift of speech, remains equally unsuccessful, so what are we to make of psyche's petulance and, in particular, of her claim that the poet knows nothing of the things that life wants? Since Hofmannsthal rethought his position and gave psyche, not the poet, the last word, one way of reading the conclusion might be to absolve the poet of guilt; after all, he tried to make psyche mindful of life's abundance before he resorted to exploring the dream medium, in which his poetic wiles play a greater role. If at this late stage psyche is still intractable, then perhaps it is because the fault lies not in life, not in the poet, not in death, but in psyche—who is somehow broken. The poet has demonstrated openness by trying to pull psyche back into the open, where there is living, and also by bringing her through dream to death, another dimension accessible to the open.

The crossing of a threshold occurs in "The Hours!" ("Die Stunden!"), and this time also there is death beyond the threshold. Hofmannsthal describes a state in which, at certain hours or certain moments, we stare out upon the bright blue of the sea "and understand death / So easily and solemnly and without dread" (*KA*, I, 49). The very deliberate wording "we . . . understand death" challenges the reader to expand his conception of both death and understanding, since "understanding" death is every bit as equivocal as "understanding" life or any other phenomenon. Two factors are operative in the first strophe; there are certain moments when, in *staring* at the bright sea, we are able to come to grips with the concept of death, and second, this coming to terms leaves us without dread.

The poet continues to elaborate on the understanding by placing the operation of death into little girls; from the stare upon the bright "bluing" of the sea ("das helle Blauen") a transition is made to our own hermeneutic inner gaze:

> Like little girls who look very pale,
> With big eyes, and who are always shivering,
> Mutely look at nothing in the evening
>
> And know that life is now flowing
> Over from their sleep-drunken limbs
> Into trees and grass, and smile a wan preening smile,
>
> Like a saint who is shedding her blood.
>
> (*KA*, I, 49)

Familiarizing death through the image of the sickly, pale girls immediately deprives death of its horror; empathy dictates that we put ourselves in their place, stand with them in the final hour on the threshold between life and death. The "understanding" of the first strophe, once so distant and unfocused, is now transferred by the poet into the minds of the dying girls; they *know* that life is abandoning them and joining with nature, and in a touching flicker of vanity the girls smilingly "preen themselves" ("und sich matt lächelnd zieren") and die like saints. Knowledge and the feeble smile both erode the horror of death, but it is even more important that life is passed on.

Death is robbed of its finality here. As Bennett explains, there is no real understanding of death, though we may have a foretaste, an an-

ticipation of it at certain receptive moments: "Whenever we feel ourselves caught up 'in the great round dance', in the totality and unity
of existence, it is essentially death's power we feel, that 'Hinüberflie-
ßen' into trees and grass which joins us to the whole of nature."[13]
Hofmannsthal actually heightens the notion of transition from life to
death to greater life by using the suggestive analogy of the saint in the
final line; saints shed their blood out of sacrifice and in anticipation of
eternal life.

Now it is possible to return to the first line and title of the poem, in
order to establish exactly what serves as the point of transition. Hofmannsthal punctuates the time factor by writing "The Hours!" We do
not know quite what to make of this unit of time; the hours could be
moments, if they are taken to mean specific intervals in greater time,
but there is also a strong indication of staring out upon the sea's
bluing *for hours* at a time, as if locked in a trance. These are the hours
"in which we stare at the bright / Bluing of the sea," so that we are
actually caught up in the activity of the sea, namely, its bluing, a syn-
esthetic operation that might be quite compelling. Like the mountain
of "We walked," the sea of this poem is giving and taking in its own
right; it is bluing as opposed to merely lying there, blue and bright.
The perception of the sea's bluing is the first hint of threshold in the
poem, and it immediately establishes an unorthodox relation between subject and world, such that we can expect the characteristic
movement and joining of the open.

Bennett points out the difference between staring and looking
(*Starren* versus *Schauen*) as it works in the poem. Insofar as we stare at
the sea there is no comprehension, because comprehension would
require seeing: "And yet, again, precisely this endless incomprehension, the collapse of experience into understanding, of 'Schauen' into
'Starren,' the repeated failure to achieve contact with death intellec-
tually, *is* the experience of mortality."[14] Now we are approaching the
meaning of the words "we understand death." At the point where
understanding breaks down, or is about to break down, we are standing on the threshold. The threshold is crossed when, in certain hours,
we "feel" or intuit the life of the sea that we are normally inclined to
view, cognitively, and this feeling or empathy with the sea induces the
staring. Staring is not necessarily not-seeing, it is in fact often a state
of having become lost, engrossed in seeing to the point where details

13. Bennett, *Hugo von Hofmannsthal*, 24.
14. *Ibid.*, 25.

of the seeing blur and dissolve. Staring is initiated by looking, by seeing, so that it is fair to say that in looking at the sea's blueness, we crossed over to a state of staring at the sea's bluing, having forgotten what we "intended" to see in the first place.

I can readily appreciate Bennett's treatment of the staring/seeing relation, and would welcome more on the subject. The receptive states so frequently captured by Hofmannsthal have a lot to do with the operation of seeing and remind me of Nietzsche's definition of seeing as a matter of seeing into abysses. In the Nietzschean conception of living, cognition is the tool of individuation. Beyond cognition at the point and at the time when cognition is enhanced and a link is forged between individual life and all life, we are no longer fixed on a specific object. Indeed, we no longer have our bearings, and that is why Nietzsche insists that man is always standing at the edge of an abyss, and that true seeing is seeing into the abyss.

Hofmannsthal does not treat the philosophical implications of seeing, which for Nietzsche would require *courage* and the fortitude to endure greater life. Instead, the poet is a sojourner, a dweller on the threshold, and his emphasis is on the experience of the journey as opposed to prescribing strategies for dealing with the abyss in order to create and maintain self despite the abyss. Still, Hofmannsthal's formidable meditation in "The Hours!" is a record of his sojourn into Nietzschean seeing; in the abyss there is death, but not only death. The death encountered in the abyss is not absolute Christian death, and the dying of little girls is not strictly speaking a Christian dying, either, because the girls' life flows into trees and grass. Hofmannsthal's experience of the abyss affords us a glimpse of the unity of individual and all, of death and life. For a moment death is allowed to dwell within us unthreateningly.

6 TRANSFORMATION

Transformation is another feature of the movement of being. In several poems Hofmannsthal allows the subject to transform, not merely to sojourn beyond the threshold. The implied return to life is common to most of the poems in which the subject crosses the threshold, into greater life ("We walked") as life, for example, or greater life as death ("The Hours!"). Upon returning, the subject's everyday life has perhaps become enriched, has perhaps been touched by profound empathy with life and death. The transitional state is not permanent—indeed, there is little "permanence" in any Hofmannsthal poem—so that it functions mainly as a portal through which the subject comes and goes in order to explore the open. In the poems illustrative of transformation, on the other hand, the subject appears to undergo a change that does not always allow a return to the initial self.

"A Boy" ("Ein Knabe") is a poem in two parts; the first part outlines the boy's youthful innocence, the second his coming of age. The obvious romantic associations, not the least of which is the motif of hyacinths in both parts of the poem, make it likely that Hofmannsthal had been inspired to some degree by Novalis' "The Apprentices at Sais," in which the protagonist Hyacinth enjoys a special intimacy with nature and achieves selfhood after completing his romantic journey.

In this allegorical fragment Novalis' protagonist undergoes a transformation similar to that of the boy in Hofmannsthal's poem. For one thing, young Hyacinth can understand the language of nature and is able to converse with animals and plants. In the social context of his human world Hyacinth remains awkward, untutored, and alienated. During Hyacinth's adolescence a stranger sojourns for a few weeks in the boy's town, relating to him all manner of tales and news of the wide world. When the stranger disappears, he leaves behind a book written in a strange language that Hyacinth is unable to read. On the advice of an old woman Hyacinth encounters in the forest, his favorite abode, he burns the book and goes out into the world to seek his fortune. He is aware of his growing love for Rosenblüte, and even the animals are aware of this change in him, but he is unable to recognize in Rosenblüte the woman of his destiny. After a journey through a romantic landscape of no specific place or time, Hyacinth's travels are rewarded when he discovers the veiled image of the goddess and, beneath that veil, his Rosenblüte. Appropriately enough, Novalis supplied his narrative with a traditional fairy-tale conclusion.[1]

Hofmannsthal's poem begins by establishing the boy's relation to his surroundings. He was not able to recognize the beauty of mussel shells, a metaphor for life, because "He was too much of one world with them" (*KA*, I, 58). The fragrance of the hyacinths meant nothing to him, and he had no concept of his own reflection or mirror image.

But the poet is careful not to paint a bleak picture of Hyacinth's boyhood; the second strophe is introduced with the familiar "yet": all the boy's days were

> Open like a lyre-shaped valley
> In which he was both master and servant
> Of the white life, without choice.
> (*KA*, I 58)

The boy's need to transcend this state is indicated in the words "without choice," for without choice there is no consciousness of self. It is the openness of the boy's condition that holds the promise of coming into selfhood, and the lyre-shaped valley in which he is lord and servant simultaneously is only a prestage of life, for "the white life" is, like whiteness, without features in the absence of color.

The third and concluding strophe of the first part describes his provisional status:

> Like one who still does what is not proper to him,
> But not for long, he walked along the paths:
> Toward homecoming and the dialogue unending
> His soul quietly lifted itself.

Having once again sounded the theme of the boy's provisional state of being, Hofmannsthal becomes more precise in defining the boy's destination. In Novalis' *Heinrich von Ofterdingen* the romantic hero is also in pursuit of home, so that homecoming takes on the allegorical

---

1. Friedrich von Hardenberg [Novalis], *Die Lehrlinge zu Sais*, in *Novalis Schriften*, ed. Paul Kluckhohn and Richard Samuel (Stuttgart, 1960), I, 91–95.

sense of achieving selfhood. Similarly, the greatest illumination on the path to spiritual maturity is initiation into the dialogue between man and world, which in Heinrich's case occurs when he meets his beloved. The union of Heinrich and Mathilde establishes totality, so that the world is no longer a detached, mute residence but a phenomenon linked to mortals through dialogue. The boy is as yet unaware that he is homeward bound, and he is not yet a participant in the endless dialogue that establishes our experience of greater life.

The dialogic aspect of being was a favorite theme among romantics.[2] Engaging in a dialogue constituted a breakthrough for the romantic imagination because the condition of solitariness was viewed as sterile. Wolfgang Nehring has outlined the ways in which one can break out of preexistence into living, and he suggests that Hofmannsthal was influenced by Novalis' writing on introspection as a starting point to breakthrough.[3] Since one of the measures by which we break through to life is by joining society and engaging in meaningful activity, it makes sense to view Novalis as a source of Hofmannsthal's thought because the romantic hero must always emerge from his introspection and alienation in order to join life. Alienation in Novalis and in the romantics in general is a provisional state superseded by joining, which is only enabled by the experience of finding oneself through introspection.

In the second part of "A Boy" we discover him changed, even as he discovers the change in himself. It is a particularly effective device that Hofmannsthal suggests, but does not illustrate, the transition; he simply divides the poem into halves and sets them off with roman numerals. It is immediately clear that the boy has been transformed:

> Before he was subdued for his fate,
> He drank much flood that was bitter and hard.
> Then strangely he rose to his feet
> And stood on the shore unusually light and empty.

The very strong wording of the opening line fills in the distance between boyhood and maturity; the boy was "subdued" for his fate ("Eh er gebändigt war"), *i.e.*, the white life is over and a taming, an imparting of direction has occurred along with the implied, and necessary, incurring of guilt. The boy has had to drink a bitter and difficult

---

2. See Del Caro, *Hölderlin*, 67–79, and Friedrich von Hardenberg [Novalis], *Heinrich von Ofterdingen*, in *Novalis Schriften*, I, 268, 287, 325.

3. Wolfgang Nehring, *Die Tat bei Hofmannsthal: Eine Untersuchung zu Hofmannsthals großen Dramen* (Stuttgart, 1966), 102–106.

"flood" (*Flut*), connoting not only the guilt readily associated with the word *flood* in its ancient biblical context but also the volume of experience that has intervened between the white and the colored life.

Of course in raising himself to his full height the boy is prepared to *see* into the world, but his first inkling is one of lightness of being. Hofmannsthal's letter to Bebenburg on November 4, 1895, three months before the writing of "A Boy," contains a relevant clarification. Hofmannsthal explained that while sojourning in Venice he looked upon the sea and comprehended, as a result of this looking, that he had aged much in the last year. Someone who is accustomed to living among houses, or in the country, is lifted above many things when he looks out upon the sea: "He feels himself clearly, but as if in air that is unusually thin. Much falls away that one had acquired as possessions, yes even as being through dream: one is uncannily light and empty" (*KA*, I, 272).

A similar experience was recorded in the poem "The Hours!", also as a result of contact with the sea. In his letter Hofmannsthal indicated that we dream ourselves into certain conditions, even dream ourselves into being, but that this inauthentic state is dispelled by joining with the sea, leaving us light and strangely empty. The boy reflects this experience as if he too were shedding the burden of dreams that posture as reality. Now he is ready to see. Mussels roll in at his feet, he is wearing hyacinths in his hair (a conscious adornment), "And their beauty he knew, and also / That this was the comfort of beautiful life," (*KA*, I, 58). Unlike the state of not-seeing in the first part, the boy's transformation enables him to perceive life's beauty and to take comfort in it. Just the need for comfort is a sign of maturity, since the boy has had to swallow much bitterness in order to arrive.

The poem's final strophe underscores the spiritual maturity of the man. Even as he knows the beauty of his surroundings, and knows himself now in relation to them by virtue of eyes that see, his life is not without ambivalence, his being not without mystery. The reader is to assume that the shells were picked up:

> Yet with an uncertain smile he soon let
> Them fall again, for one great look
> At these pretty dungeons showed him
> His own incomprehensible fate.
>
> (*KA*, I, 58)

These lines represent the highest, most poignant experience of life, and they function poetically both as the seal and the open end of the poem. The mussel shells are beautiful, yes, and they are a source of comfort, but essentially the shells are dungeons containing life, just as in "real life" they are not pretty shells for our aesthetic taste but the armor and abode of tiny *living* sea animals.

The shells that are washed upon the shore no longer dwell within their proper medium—they become mere shells, and their "beauty" is as nonliving objects. The waves that carry the shells to the shore are the waves of transitoriness, for in their arms the waves carry a message to the man of his own fate, his own mortality: This beauty *was* life, this beauty *is* life, but it will fade and so will you. The man lets the shells drop because he has the insight of his own imprisonment, his own transitoriness, and it is a masterful poetic device to have the sea function as the carrying, sustaining metaphor. The shells first thrive in the sea, then they are given up by the sea and pass over into their "next life," namely, the life of animating human life that stands on the shore. Hofmannsthal associated the sea with passing, with death subsumed in life, and nowhere does he accomplish this fusion with greater effect than in "A Boy."

In the context of "Nox Portentis Gravida" Hofmannsthal had penned these notes concerning the prison motif: "Misery. Each person is imprisoned in himself, harnessed to the plow of his life, stuck inside the *ergastulum* of his body . . . how do we wrest life from its dungeons?" (*KA*, I, 281). The word *Kerker,* meaning "dungeons," was used at the conclusion of "A Boy," and in the above note Hofmannsthal used the verb *einkerkern* to connote the act of locking someone in a dungeon. The Latin *ergastulum* was a dungeon on a Roman farm used to confine slaves. The individual, according to Hofmannsthal, is imprisoned not necessarily by the physicality of the body, since the senses are what enable us to achieve insight; instead, it appears that individual limitations (oneself, one's life, one's body) are the dungeon: we "have" only one life, but are cognizant of life everywhere.

Another transformation of a boy occurs in "The Young Man in the Landscape" ("Der Jüngling in der Landschaft"), which at one time had been titled "Life Songs of the Plowmen" ("Der Pflüger Lebenslieder") (*KA*, I, 302). The ambivalence of the title, as well as the alternate title, points to a joining of life with land. The youth is not juxtaposed with the landscape, he is *in it,* he is part of the landscape, living in it and sharing its life. Plowmen who sing of life, moreover, are not philosophers but simple persons whose intimate contact with the land enables them to sing of life: they know the land, the land is life, they sing of life. These plowmen are the original, primitive lyricists.

The activities of lines 1–8 describe, not the youth, but instead the landscape and its dwellers. The scene opens with gardeners laying open their beds, preparing the soil of their plots, but is soon expanded to include the presence of beggars everywhere. These beggars are described both as foreboding, "With eyes bound in black, and with crutches," and as hopeful, "Yet also with harps and the new flowers, / The strong scent of fragile spring flowers" (*KA*, I, 65). The cycle of life is contained in these lines, with gardeners preparing to sow and the beggars out hawking their early flowers. The other contrast is between domesticity and homelessness.

The images are greatly expanded in lines 6–8:

> The naked trees set everything free:
> One saw down the river and saw the market
> And many children playing beside ponds.
>
> (*KA*, I, 65)

A special view is afforded by the naked trees, so that the impersonal "one" is able to look down the length of the river, see the market, see children playing along the way. The landscape is unusually open at this point, and here the subject enters the poem.

> Through this landscape he slowly walked
> And felt its power and knew, that
> The world's destinies related to him.

On his walk *through* the wide-open landscape the subject is able to feel its power, and he also has knowledge of his complicity in the world's events; experience of the land here connects the youth to world. But even this "experience" of the land is qualified, since it is not the experience of those who dwell in the land—the gardeners, beggars, and children.

As one who comes from without, that is, from outside the landscape, the traveler establishes his relation to the world through the landscape. He is now ready to undergo a transformation:

> Toward those strange children he now walked
> And was prepared, on a threshold unknown
> To spend a new life in service.

The traveler comes to the unknown threshold with the experience of the land, which we may assume is a new experience on the part of one who was an outsider, and his first direction is to approach the playing children in order to enter a new life of service. All three lines contain or imply transition: the children will not always be children, the subject feels readiness at an unknown threshold, and the nature of the readiness is to lead a new life.

The transformation is difficult to apprehend because the reader does not know where the subject came from, who the subject is, etc. In fact, interpretative speculation on the subject's identity would not yield much. Hofmannsthal tells us something about him in the concluding strophe, but even this information underscores the irrelevance of the subject's prior dwelling and station in life. The entire previous inventory of his soul, we are told, is now regarded by the subject as nothing more than "worthless possession" ("nichtigen Besitz"):

> Only the fragrance of flowers spoke to him now
> Of strange beauty, and the new air
> He inhaled in silence but without longing
> Only that he was allowed to serve pleased him.
>
> (KA, I, 65)

The reader is of course invited to assume that before his transformation the subject was not a servant, that he stood in some exterior, perhaps even some exploitative relation to the land. Now, however, the transformed subject is able to sense the land without disposing of his experience judgmentally; the flowers "speak" of strange beauty and he calmly breathes the new air, but he does not exhibit any longing for these things—they are in him. His willingness and pleasure at being "allowed" to serve may, in fact, amount to nothing more than the understanding of a traveler who experiences the paradoxical humility of total kinship with the earth. This illumination ties him to the destinies of the world, yes, but not in such a way that he will become a world mover; it is the permission to spend his new life in service that is the true liberating factor.

In "A Boy" the subject was liberated from the "white life," *i.e.,* the life of not-seeing, and the transformation took him to manhood and full understanding of morality. In "The Young Man in the Landscape," liberation occurs, paradoxically, when the youth realizes his kinship with the land, becomes part of the landscape, and has a mind only to serve. Hofmannsthal elaborated on the motif of self/land conflation in "Message" ("Botschaft"), a poem in which the familiar Hölderlinian motif of *Geselligkeit, i.e.,* conviviality, is used as a vehicle of transformation.

The poem begins with a resolute thesis: Only those days may be called the best days "when conversingly we / Transformed the landscape before our eyes / Into a realm of the soul" (*KA*, I, 78). Prerequisites for our best days are: being together, engaging in dialogue, seeing the landscape, and allowing the landscape into the dialogue in such a way that, in all its multifariousness, it becomes a realm of the soul ("ein Reich der Seele"). Hofmannsthal next enumerates features of this soul landscape. The friends climb up to a grove lying in shadow, and it receives them "like something previously experienced." On isolated meadows they are able to "find" the dream of life of beings never divined.[4] Hovering somehow over the pond, the friends discover "a gliding dialogue / Reflecting an arch deeper still than the sky" (*KA*, I, 78). All these properties of the soul landscape are perceived after the initial transformation of the friends' souls into landscape, and they all bear the marks of experience beyond the threshold.

Especially illustrative of the open here is the quality of the pond: Above it hovers a "gliding dialogue" ("gleitendes Gespräch") whose effect, heightened by synesthesia, reflects or reveals an arch that is even deeper than the arch of the heavens when they stretch above us. Under normal conditions the distance that lies between earth and sky is vast indeed, and we are moved by such distance, perhaps to reflect upon ourselves in the vastness of the universe. Hofmannsthal frequently remarked in his poems and observations upon the special quality of light reflected off bodies of water toward evening; there is a joining between heaven and earth visible to the eye as reflection. The transformed landscape gives off or radiates a gliding dialogue—a dialogue that is not static—illustrative of the open relation prevailing between pond and sky and illustrative also of the friends' ability to hear and see this dialogue and to share in its openness.

The poet reiterates the thesis at precisely midpoint in the poem:

> Only one thing avails: to be convivial with friends.
> So I want you to come and drink with me
> From those pitchers that are my inheritance.
>
> (*KA*, I, 78)

---

4. See "A Dream of Great Magic," where dream exists somewhere and we are capable of finding it, but not necessarily capable of "having" it or dreaming it.

Compare this passage from Hölderlin's "Bread and Wine," strophe 3, in which he invites the reader out into the open: "Divine fire also drives us, by day and by night, / To move on. So come! that we may look upon the open."[5] Hölderlin's "divine fire" is wine, enjoyed in the conviviality of friendship, and it functions very much like the catalyst for transformation occurring in Hofmannsthal's poetics.

This sharing of friendship goes beyond merely sitting in the presence of another; indeed, Hofmannsthal invites the friend to share with him all that he was, in the sense of ancestors, and all that he *will be*, in the sense of heirs. The device that will enable this intimacy of sharing, this conviviality beyond the present and into even remote future, is suggested in the analogy of the landscape. The friend will see Hofmannsthal's landscape spread before him, even when they are apart, and recognize in the landscape traces, features of himself, of the friend. Hofmannsthal even suggests a holy communion, as Hölderlin before him, by having the friends partake of the special drink.

The individual friend dissolves or diffuses initially when the landscape, normally out there, is taken in by the two in such a way that landscape becomes soul. In this state the friends explore dimensions of themselves, and one another, as if they were able to traverse wondrous landscapes in which the dialogic powers of conviviality are at their peak. As if to further liberate the individual, the fixed ego that must always stand in the way of joining, of exploring the open, Hofmannsthal allows the substance of the friend to become liquid and in that form pass into the other's veins, animating the friend with his own otherwise inaccessible essence. It is thus on many levels of meaning that the title "Message" comes through. Message here is not merely nor primarily a linguistic medium, but a living and sustaining survival of contact through transformation, bringing us back to the thesis that "the most beautiful days" are not temporally circumscribed moments of the past but days of fruitful wandering about in the soul landscape that endures.

Hofmannsthal's final lyrical treatment of the theme of transformation occurs in the late poem "Transformation" ("Verwandlung"), from 1902. The poem is a freely translated and somewhat expanded version of Coleridge's "Phantom or Fact," and like Coleridge's poem contains a dialogue with roles ascribed to the poet and a friend.[6] The poet

5. Friedrich Hölderlin, "Brod und Wein," in *Gedichte nach 1800* (Stuttgart, 1951), 91, Vol. II, Pt. 1 of *Hölderlin: Sämtliche Werke*, ed. Friedrich Beissner.

6. See *KA*, I, 411, for the text of Coleridge's poem, or *The Complete Poetical Works of Samuel Taylor Coleridge*, ed. E. H. Coleridge (3rd ed.; Oxford, 1962), 484–85.

describes how he is visited by "a lovely image" who silently looks at him and has a captivating effect upon him: "That sweet dread ran through my marrow, / And I grasped: this is my true self" (*KA*, I, 103). The poet welcomes this appearance of his perceived true self ("mein wahres Ich") and even feels nourished by his gaze, but suddenly the image turns away from him and adopts strange features that become hardened under the poet's weary gaze:

> And now—his face did not come back to him—
> And yet: stranger staring at the strange,
> I felt inside, persisting in my madness,
> A knowledge seated deep and unmoving:
> This is not the strange, rather this am I.
> (*KA*, I, 103)

It is troublesome to speak of a transformation in the first instance, because the image suddenly appears and bears the features of the poet, and he, quite moved, assumes the image to be his true self. Transformation takes place when the image and the poet exchange looks, as they are looking at each other, for then the image transforms into a stranger, or better, into a strange thing or "the strange" ("ein Fremdes"). A second, inner transformation takes place when the poet, staring at the strange thing, poignantly realizes it is he after all.

When it is the friend's turn to speak, he asks if this enigma is supposed to deal with reality, if it is supposed to yield something or only delude. The friend demands to know at least in what time frame this "appalling transformation" took place. The poet's response:

> Confined to the space of a moment
> It is a crumbling nothing from the land of dreams.
> But assume that years have passed you darkly,
> You see what every life conceals within itself.

The poet's answer is equivocal, suggesting that questions about reality, delusion, time are not helpful here. If the entire episode *could* have taken place within an isolated moment, then, apparently, the whole thing was a fragment of interference from the realm of dream, a virtual nothing. But the conditional nature of the poet's response holds out the possibility that one's entire life could have been consumed by this process of transformation. If one's life passes in darkness, without knowledge of oneself, then time itself has not been perceived properly. But there is also the notion that each person's life has the potential to present him with such a phantom, if the years are allowed to work (*wirken*) darkly and unheeded.

Hofmannsthal's interest in rewriting Coleridge's poem was quite understandable, since he had been concerned with the concept of self and selfhood for many years by the time he wrote "Transformation." Selfhood is the condition that we must strive for in breaking out of preexistence, and selfhood should be a state of openness and seeing, not merely a condition of individuation. In this poem, the subject is visited by a phantom perceived to be the subject's true self; in the early stage of the transformation a lesser and true self coexist. Before the lesser self has time to do anything but thoroughly enjoy the presence of his true self, *i.e.*, before he has time to decide what to do about either himself or his phantom "true self" (which one will continue?), the true self transforms into a strange thing and the lesser self loses himself, becoming a stranger staring at a strange thing. In the second stage of the transformation the lesser self transforms into a stranger, and the true self transforms into a strange thing. Finally, paradoxical as it is, the unselved lesser self discovers himself again by realizing who the transformed true self is—indeed, at this point it is futile to talk about different selves, for there is integration, only one self.

Perhaps "Transformation" is an allegory of the stages of life, or an intensified experience of self-doubling and ascent to true selfhood. In any case, the poem is consistent with Hofmannsthal's views on selfhood as expressed in the essay "Dialogue on Poems" (1903). It is relevant to note that "Transformation" is related in dialogue form also, perhaps because Hofmannsthal understood that in order to explore the self, a vantage point outside the self must be near, to function as a surface for the self's echo, or to function as a threshold for the coming and going that Hofmannsthal attributed to the open.

These words are spoken by Gabriel to Clemens as he is trying to explain that in order to find self, we must not restrict ourselves to searching within; on the contrary, we are to be found "outside" (*draußen*): "We do not possess our self: from outside it blows upon us, it flees from us for a long time and returns to us in a breath. To be sure—our 'self'! The word is really such a metaphor. Stirrings return that at some earlier time nested here. And are they really the same ones anymore? It is not instead their brood that is driven back here by some dark homing instinct?" (*Prosa II*, 83). This sophisticated understanding of the nature of self is entirely in keeping with Hofmannsthal's striving in the poetry to establish and maintain the open; no wonder, then, that in discovering the self he resorts to operations that linger always on the threshold, remain open always to sentiments and experiences that return as if by virtue of some dark homing instinct ("einem dunklem Heimatgefühl").

The term *self* is a metaphor for what is ostensibly ours, in the sense of *proprium*, but is at liberty to flee and return in *transformed state* because it has experienced selfhood on its own, in communion with the world, and for this reason can never be said to belong to us exclusively. The integrity of self is as tenuous as the *principium individuationis* once that state has been notified of the greater life which subsumes it. But I do not think that in harboring these thoughts Hofmannsthal is pessimistic about the possibilities of achieving selfhood. To the extent that we are able to "reclaim" or recognize the impulses that return to us, we are in a position to assert our selves in the world, to wrest that much life from the vast thronging of life. The goal is not to strive for some perfect quantum of life but to delimit and maintain a living self that has been harvested from the source, the mother lode, while keeping a mindful, living commerce with the source.

Movement across the threshold and movement within the animated landscape of the open takes many shapes. Sometimes heightened receptivity enables the subject to "experience" dimensions of the open such as art, death, union with the land. At other times, inexplicably and seemingly without transition, a transformation occurs; notable in these transformations is the presence of life after the subject has transformed, but without a record of the intervening life ("A Boy" and "Transformation"). There is also a state of homelessness connoting movement across the threshold, though an equally valid phrase might be "at home everywhere." For this is the problem we find, to some extent, in Hofmannsthal's celebrated poem "Song of Life" ("Lebenslied").

"Song of Life" provoked a rash of criticism and interpretation owing to its alleged incomprehensibility (*KA*, I, 291–97), and it continued to receive close attention in the somewhat un-Nietzschean monograph by Richard Exner, and the pro-Nietzschean book by Meyer-Wendt.[7] I am concerned mostly with the activity of the heir in "Song of Life" and the heir's ability, despite having to deal with *inherited* abundance, to move about freely, *as if* he were homeless and without

---

7. Exner, *Hofmannsthals "Lebenslied,"* 67; Meyer-Wendt, *Der frühe Hofmannsthal,* 39, 43–44.

history. The following information concerning a concrete source for Hofmannsthal's poem should preface, but not necessarily limit, any discussion of it.

Hofmannsthal's acquaintance, a certain Alice Morrison, related to him how she lived for a time in India. She was a guest one evening of a prominent host who lived in a palacelike structure adjoining a zoological garden. In the hot evening she went out onto the balcony overlooking the garden, and she was able to distinguish the vague, moving shapes of all kinds of exotic animals, birds, quadrupeds, and reptiles. At this point she was overcome by a "powerful mystic-pantheistic feeling of all-connectedness" (*Allverbundenheit*), and in order to intensify this moment even more, she opened a phial of perfume that she had inherited from her grandmother and sprinkled drops of the precious scent upon the animals below.[8] In "Song of Life" Hofmannsthal has the heir "squandering" his inheritance, an ointment (*Salböl*), on eagle, lamb, and peacock. Exner quite properly refuses to question the veracity or authenticity of the woman's story, and he admits that the poem's first image rests on a concrete basis. But Exner also perceives that this basis, in itself and examined in its own right, is not very concrete.[9] Hofmannsthal did not need to change anything connected with this image because he was able to relate the event to his own experience and his own poetic.

The factual basis of the opening image of "Song of Life" does nothing to detract from the wealth of associations that Hofmannsthal evokes, so that Exner's purpose in devoting an entire book to the poem is easily appreciated. He writes, "I wish to comprehend 'Song of Life' as a sum and center of emanation, as a poem in which nearly all the lines of the early work intersect, and at the same time as a text that still resounds in the later and latest works of Hofmannsthal."[10] This admirable objective is well demonstrated using the example of "Song of Life," but I am interested in particular in the *movements* of the heir as they relate to the threshold motif.

The poem opens with an animated, open-ended image; the heir is squandering on animals the ointment that he has received "from the hands / Of the dead old woman" (*KA*, I, 63). The first line contains an implied subject with implied address: "Let the heir squander" ("Den Erben lass verschwenden") could be addressed to us, as readers, but more likely to the anonymous posterity of mankind. We are told not

8. Exner, *Hofmannsthals "Lebenslied,"* 84–85; also printed in *KA*, I, 295–96.
9. Exner, *Hofmannsthals "Lebenslied,"* 85.
10. *Ibid.*, 19.

to be overly concerned about what the heir does with his inheritance; we should allow him his freedom in this matter, since his nature is quite open.

The departing dead and the treetops of the distance are to him of equal value with the steps of lady dancers. Clearly, the heir possesses special powers and is not limited; death and nature do not preoccupy him. In fact, he has received his inheritance from the hands of a dead woman, constituting not a paradox, as Meyer-Wendt explains, but "a temporal blending into the past as it can only be expressed by Hofmannsthal."[11] The heir's position in the giving/taking relation is interesting; an inheritance connects the dead with the living, pulling "out of the hands" of the dead a substance to be squandered in life. The whole idea of heir and inheritance challenges the finality of death and underscores the "temporal blending" and crossing back and forth between life and death that is possible for the heir and, apparently, to a limited degree is also possible for the ancestor: The dead old woman *hands* him the ointment. It is as if Hofmannsthal were saying that the dead are more constrained by the conventions of space and time than are the living, but still able to participate in the moment of transition embodied in the gesture of passing on the inheritance.

The heir's autonomy of movement is highlighted in the second strophe; he walks like one who is not threatened by a power from behind, not threatened by the past. Confronted by life's wrinkles or by mortality, he is able to smile:

> To him each place offers
> Secretly its threshold,
> To every way he gives
> Himself, the homeless one!
> (*KA*, I, 63)

Meyer-Wendt proposes a reading of these lines with which I cannot agree; because the heir gives himself to every wave, the experiential realm of the heir is supposed to be the outer, visible world of appearance.[12] If this were the case, what are we to make of the heir's gift enabling him to cross the threshold of every place? When Hofmannsthal writes that each place (*Stelle*) secretly offers its threshold to the heir, it is because the heir cannot—will not—be arrested in his movements. It makes no sense to insist that his experience is exhausted in the world of appearance, since he is able to *escape* all ap-

11. Meyer-Wendt, *Der frühe Hofmannsthal*, 43–44.
12. *Ibid.*, 45.

pearance by virtue of not having to reside or endure in any particular place. The image of the threshold is another way of saying that permanence, which is always only a seeming permanence, does not delude him.

Additional images of movement include the swarm of wild bees that takes along his soul, the singing of dolphins that speeds his steps, and the whole earth bearing him "With powerful gestures" (*KA*, I, 63). Hofmannsthal concludes the poem by repeating the image of the first strophe, but this time he adds the modifier "smilingly" to the heir's squandering, and he rearranges lines 1–4 of the poem.[13] The poem then concludes:

> He smiles to his companions,—
> The hovering weightless
> Abysses and the gardens
> Of life carry him!
>
> (*KA*, I, 63)

Hofmannsthal used the exclamation point six times in the poem, heightening the effect of the heir's activities and abilities, as if to underscore their wondrous nature. Teaming up with the dead, as it were, enables the heir to traverse life under special power; he is not constrained by the inheritance but enabled by it, in the sense that someone who inherits a fortune may indeed live uninhibitedly. The heir's capacity to squander his inherited ointment on animals, each of which has symbolic importance that I will not explore, is a statement regarding how he will live *his* life.

The ointment may have been precious indeed, since the dead old woman passed it on to the heir; in her life she preserved it, letting her own life flow into it, and in death she wished her life to continue in the heir's. But the heir must not feel constrained to cherish this ointment as the woman did—how could he be a mere clone of her? In his animation and fortification as heir—that is, as recipient of a precious life potion—he is endowed with an abundance that must be squandered, even as Nietzsche insisted, and Hofmannsthal well knew, that it is in the nature of life to squander, to discharge, *not* to hold back. One who is so empowered by the ancestors, to use Hofmannsthal's analogy, participates in the "song of life" by spending what he is and remaining always in the open.

Up to this point I have concentrated on dynamic expressions of

13. The new arrangement stresses in this order: (1) the ointment, (2) from the dead woman's hands, (3) he smilingly squanders, and (4) on eagle, lamb, and peacock.

experience beyond the threshold, with the exception of "From Aboard Ship," where Hofmannsthal revealed that the poet is not always as footloose and enterprising as the heir of "Song of Life." The receptivity required to engage the open life is not always present, and in the absence of movement into life, we sometimes persist in dwelling in separate, unconnected chambers, chambers like the dungeons of shells that I discussed in connection with "A Boy." In one of his longest and darkest poems Hofmannsthal depicted this isolated, unpenetrating mode of existence and detailed the apocalyptic manner in which life erupts to explode all boundaries.

"Nox Portentis Gravida" emerged as the title of a poem for which Hofmannsthal had also considered the title "Nox Tripartita."[14] If we translate the Latin roughly as "A Night Filled with Portents" or "filled with foreboding," it will become apparent why Hofmannsthal also gave thought to calling the poem "A Night in Three Parts." The poem is divided into three parts, each reflecting a different realm and degree of life. But Hofmannsthal did not intend these realms to suggest authenticity within themselves; in his notes he wrote: "Nox portentis gravida appears to tear the world into three totally unrelated realms: the realm of unknowing nature, falsely called the 'eternally cheerful'; on the other hand [the realm of] innocence" (KA, I, 280). In these notes Hofmannsthal referred only to the first two realms, since the third realm is the encompassing one. I place great significance on the use of the word "appears" because the poet explodes this appearance even as he presents his text in three strophes.

Under the cover of night's darkness the first scene points to the sky and establishes a mythological tone. As the mist rises into the tall trees, three beautiful stars glitter close-by. The hyacinths on the dark ground "Remember that something will happen here, / That happened earlier and frequently" (KA, I, 59). The event of the future that has its origins in the past concerns Hermes and the two Dioscuri, Castor and Pollux; twinkling boldly they will surround the airy paths of the windborne Graces, and

> Playingly, with the cruelty of the hunt,
> Scare them from the treetops, yes drive
> Them to the river's waves, till it dawns.
> (KA, I, 59)

14. See KA, I, 280, for possible sources in Goethe and Kleist.

This event from the past repeated into the future is Hofmannsthal's invention, insofar as there is no evidence in Greek literature for such an encounter between Hermes and the Dioscuri (*KA*, I, 280). And this is precisely Hofmannsthal's point, namely, that man's mythologized and mythologizing position vis-à-vis nature attributes a false cheerfulness to it. We love to see our belief in regularity, in order, in cosmos, reflected in the appearance of the constellations, for in this manner, nature is innocuous.

Beneath his own part of heaven the poet of the second strophe looks but does not see:

> The poet elsewhere has his road,
> And looking with the eyes of medusa
> He sees the surrounding fallow field
> At once displaced, and knows not how things are,
> And adds it to other such places
> Where his soul, hidden like a child,
> Has existence of no certain term
> In eagle's air and calm long dead.
> There he strews shadows and appearances for it
> Of the earth's things, and precious stones.
>
> (*KA*, I, 59)

The poet's realm is one of innocence, as this idea was explored in connection with "Where little cliffs . . ." ("Wo kleine Felsen . . ."). In that poem Hofmannsthal maintained that the poets, "drunk with poems," have greater innocence than children engaging in play, because the poets remained untouched by life. He also made specific reference to "Where little cliffs . . ." in order to illustrate the innocent realm of the second strophe of "Nox" (*KA*, I, 280).

The medusa stare that is capable of turning people into stone is an effective transition from the inauthentic, idealized realm of nature to the poet's instrumentality in viewing the world in this way. Hofmannsthal says, "The poet elsewhere has his road," but it is the poet who has created the mythologies and the myths of a cheerful nature, so that he is described as having the qualities of one of his mythological figures. Where the poet looks, everything lies fallow and seems displaced, so that he flees into his ephemeral existence, his soul hiding like a child and in need of the pretty illusions he scatters before it; this poet of innocence is apparently successful in wooing psyche, but, on the other hand, this poet's psyche has no appetite for life.

The realm of nature and the realm of the poet should not be divided, and this Hofmannsthal demonstrates by allowing the mythological associations of Part 1 to spill over into Part 2. If the poets had not attributed "eternal cheerfulness" to nature by casting it in a desired image of man, then perhaps the poets would not be timid children who console themselves with baubles. Authentic existence—the higher existence or greater, open life championed by Hofmannsthal—requires the loss of innocence; actions and works, not dreams, create a bond with the living.

The implied criticism of the poet is embedded within the first two images of the third strophe. The third part of the sky, Hofmannsthal writes, is taken up by a cloud of such deathly black "As falls upon the soul of he who / Seeks his way at night with a candle" (*KA*, I, 59). This is not "cheerful" nature anymore, this is supremely indifferent nature darkening the way of the lost soul. At this point Hofmannsthal allows the night to disgorge itself of its portents, to give birth in the Latin sense of *gravida* as pregnant. The eruption takes place not at night, however, but on the next morning, appropriately signaling the transition that simultaneously subsumes the artificially divorced realms.

The awesome cloud is filled with thousands of thunderbolts, with flashing lightning "strong as nearby suns," and it afflicts the island with its horrific avalanche of hot stones. Meanwhile, on the island, a volcanic eruption is taking place, so that Hofmannsthal allows the visitation from above to conflate with the eruption below; thunderbolts, lightning, and molten rock rain down upon the people. Now we are given the point of view of the island's inhabitants; the tremendous quaking about them

> Let blossom the most wonderful ecstasies;
> Weeping stilled only by awesome fear
> Was the price: that in devastated gardens
> Those who never saw themselves found their way to life
> And dying drunkenly, desired no salvation;
> That God escaped the bonds of air and earth,
> Orphaned children glowed like prophets
> And all souls blossomed like the stars.
>
> (*KA*, I, 59–60)

Perhaps most puzzling, on the surface, is the poet's insistence that this cataclysm inspired wonderful ecstasies in the people. A glance into Hofmannsthal's notes illuminates this strange reaction.

Within the context of "A Boy" I discussed earlier how the beautiful "dungeons" of that poem, *i.e.*, the colorful shells that wash up on shore, serve as metaphors of the man's mortality—they used to house lives, and mortals are also imprisoned within their shells and do not always live. In his notes to "Nox" Hofmannsthal raised this question: How is it possible to tear life from its dungeons? (*KA*, I, 281). The divided realms of "Nox" are illustrative of the imprisonment that does not allow life in, and does not allow life out. Nature and art (the poet), frequently perceived as separate realms, cannot in reality exist in separation—one animates the other, and mortals should be free to come and go in the open that is broad enough to encompass both; indeed, "broad enough" is a mere figure of speech, for the nature of the open is open.

Hofmannsthal shatters these insular realms, or rather, he blasts them with a powerful eruption of nature from above and below; the tripartite night unleashes its fury, and the elements are no longer stable; heaven and earth conjoin to visit their destruction upon humans. The open realm encompasses human society, nature, and art—it does not offer eternal bliss or the innocent musings of the poet. Mortals, moreover, stand to gain from this horrible event because they are torn out of their dungeons, out of their trancelike existence, *into an immediate and unmitigated presence of life.* It is this presence of life, albeit it in the urgent sensing of human life endangered by calamity, that allows the "islanders" to experience ecstasy in the midst of their terror.

At this stage a brief recounting of Kleist's novella *The Earthquake in Chile* will help to establish Hofmannsthal's mood. A young man, Jeronimo, fathers a child, out of wedlock, with his beloved Josepha. In the moments before the earthquake, she is to be executed, even as the young man awaits his fate in a dungeon. When the earthquake occurs, he is miraculously freed from his cell, the young lady is miraculously freed from her execution, and she manages to rescue her baby. The two find each other again in the open countryside to which the survivors of the quake have fled. A general euphoria knits the survivors together; apparently, old wounds and old sins are forgotten and forgiven. In the Eden-like qualities of the country, people help one another and the young couple believes that fate has intervened in their behalf. They try to preserve their anonymity and look forward to starting a new life in Spain, just as everyone else looks forward to living anew now that they have savored the sweetness of life after having experienced hell. However, the sentiments of the country are transferred back to the city when someone suggests that a thanksgiving mass be offered.

When the community gathers again at the cathedral and prepares to give thanks, the young couple is recognized and denounced, and the quake is blamed on them. Jeronimo and Josepha are clubbed to death, and even the baby Josepha happens to be holding, though it is not her own, is torn from her arms and smashed against the cathedral wall. In an instant the madness of society's hatred is restored, and the healing virtues of the natural catastrophe vanish. The parentless child, however, is adopted by a couple who had befriended the unfortunate young people during the Eden phase of the disaster.[15]

Purchased at the expense of their awesome fear and sorrow, the people of Hofmannsthal's poem derived benefits from the disaster. For some who had never had an inkling of their true selves, the disaster made them believers in life; they "found their way to life" in one glorious moment and, dying in their intoxication with life, did not even desire salvation. The one overwhelming draught of life apparently sufficed for an entire lifetime. And consider these words from "Dialogue on Poems": Gabriel explains to Clemens that the power to experience sacrifice symbolically comes from the fact that "we and the world are not different things." Clemens is distressed by this view, so Gabriel elaborates by saying that man's oneness with the world is really "infinitely calming. It is singularly sweet to see a part of one's gravity being removed, and even if it were only for the mystical term of one breath. In our body the All is coiled together and stifled: how blissful to relieve the terrible pressure a thousandfold" (*Prosa II*, 90). It is in the spirit of the "All uncoiling within us" that the dying victims do not crave further life. God, too, was liberated from the dungeon of air and earth to which society had confined him; no longer would He have to dwell beyond, in the heavens, no longer would his worship be limited to the earthly cathedrals and convents. Orphaned children, the chaff of humanity, otherwise abandoned to an existence of poverty, begging, or crime, now "glow like prophets," their beauty abundantly radiant and visible to all. And finally, all souls blossom like the stars.

The image of souls bursting forth or blossoming like the stars is particularly suggestive, and it brings us full circle to the night scene established in Part 1. But we sense that there is no returning to that cheerful, mythologized night sky because the intervening events have covered us all with authentic night, with the one night.

15. Heinrich von Kleist, *Das Erdbeben in Chili*, in *Werke in einem Band*, ed. Helmut Sembdner (Munich, 1966), 687–99.

Returning now to Hofmannsthal's question: How can life be wrested from its dungeons? It is plain that in some cases extremely drastic intervention is required to blast mortals from their complacency, from their absolute lethargy.[16] Human life tends to grow in on itself, tends to weave a cocoon around itself, so that a powerful inoculation is required to bring humans up to the status of the living. But this is not all Hofmannsthal had to say in connection with the natural disaster, and if it were, the poem would resemble too much a theodicy. True, life unleashes its forces upon the unliving and pulls them out of their shells, but many of the "converts" are too broken to contain life anymore, and in any case, the ecstatic syndrome attaching to the postdisaster living and dying cannot endure as the measure of human life, it cannot survive in the long run.

I think there is a warning in "Nox" against letting life ebb to such a point that only a disaster can spark it up. This warning is included in lines 32–33: "Weeping stilled only by awesome fear / Was the price" (*KA*, I, 60). The extraordinary displays of vitality were bought at a price, that price being of course great human suffering. It seems not to matter whether the quantum of life is squandered in a moment, as with the dying victims, or ebbs away slowly, for in either case the price is death. Hofmannsthal attributed these words to Fortunio in a draft for a play:

> Life bears within it an unshakable law, and each thing has its price: on love stands the pain of love, on the happiness of achievement the unending wariness along the way. . . . On existence itself stands the price of death.—But all this infinitely finer, infinitely more real than words can say.—No one can get around this; incessantly each person pays with his being, and so no one can purchase something higher than he deserves for a cheaper price. And this reaches into death: fate smashes brows of marble with a diamond club, it uses a withered branch to crush the brows of dirt. (*KA*, I, 168)

Clearly revealed in the words of Fortunio is the law of fate dictating that each gets his own, and each gets nothing for free. What are we to make of this seemingly grim, seemingly deterministic observation? How do Fortunio's words square with the generous and wondrous open that Hofmannsthal explored?

In the open there is freedom for the seeing, for the living, as long as they possess the strength to move on and explore the open; the

16. Precedents exist in Hölderlin, Heine, and Nietzsche; all used the motif of lightning as a mediating or inoculating device to rouse the spirit.

distance one may traverse and the experiences one may have depend on the quality or strength of that person's life, his capacity for moving. In the example of the heir in "Song of Life" Hofmannsthal presents a figure who is seemingly omnipotent, but judging by the words of Fortunio, the heir's travels will come to an end; life will not carry him forever on its waves—the heir is not immortal. No heir is immortal, since he takes his strength from ancestors and squanders their energy and his own.

In the case of the island inhabitants of "Nox Portentis Gravida," there would have been no experience of the open whatsoever, but for the fact that their unspeakable suffering *bought* them a moment of glorious living. In their case, apparently, a moment was all they earned, all they had a right to, and its dizzying glory was commensurate with the horrible collapse of their outer lives, their trance lives. They got out of life, as the saying goes, what they put into it, though they only began to put anything into life at the very threshold of death, when it was too late.

So "Nox" is not a theodicy; the poem does not defend the omnipotence and goodness of Life in the face of natural disasters. Indeed, "life" should not be written as "Life," as though it were God, because Hofmannsthal's conception of life is such that it, life, liberates God from the dungeons mortals attribute to God. This same God was present, ostensibly, during the unliving duration of the islanders' existence, yet God did not bring them life. Life came upon—fell upon—the islanders, liberating both them and their God. Life has no motivations, no plan, no special affinity for humans; humans, on the other hand, cultivate a special affinity for life, and each gets his measure.

It would be a rather closed, inert life, after all, if life conformed to the specifications of our longing. There can be no genuine movement across the threshold if what lies beyond the threshold bears the features and proportions of our making; what we make ensnares us. Even our selves, as Hofmannsthal wrote in "Dialogue on Poems," are not possessed by us; *self* is the metaphor for an aggregate of sensations that return after having nested in us for a time, and the returning sensations are not the same ones anyway but the hatchlings of the earlier sensations. We cannot expect to have anything for free, according to Fortunio, so why should we expect to have unlimited life, or life without a price?

The open is free in the sense that once having gained access to the open life, the individual is free to squander his measure there. But the open is not free in the sense of being without a price; both notions of freedom taken as absolutes are meaningless, and would overturn the definition of open. We cannot exhaust the open life, cannot span it or control it, unless we try to fool ourselves like the innocent poet of "Nox"; his soul hides like a child whom he must coax out of hiding with pretty things of his making. In order for the open life to remain a factor, we must recognize that as beings we are part of the open, but subject to the unshakable law of life. We do not transcend life, we do not in a strict sense even transcend self. On truly good days we are liberated from our beautiful shells.

7 TIME

The *fin de siècle,* according to Jens Malte Fischer, was carried primarily by a consciousness arising from its authors' special proclivity for aesthetics and their common social background, resulting in the expression of a "sub-sensual world." This separate world became an esoteric enclave "with quasi hermetic secret knowledge" accessible only to those who were sufficiently educated and linguistically skilled to read the French standard-bearers in the original.[1] This statement probably stands up well as a very general description of the period, and certainly Hofmannsthal was enormously aided in his writings of the 1890s by virtue of his proficiency in the major European languages.

Equally important to writers of Hofmannsthal's generation was the consciousness of naturalism, that movement anchored so firmly in contemporary life that in Germany its major proponents espoused a narrow, restrictive view of art subsumed in the formula "art = nature − x."[2] Hofmannsthal's writings represented a vigorous alternative to naturalism, for he understood art not as a vehicle for depicting social conditions and championing social issues but as the vehicle per se of life as life is articulated in and by humans. In this profound sense, I entirely agree with Meyer-Wendt, who writes, "it was already an achievement of a special nature [that Hofmannsthal] was able to recognize in Nietzsche a necessary alternative to his age."[3] The alternative Hofmannsthal recognized in Nietzsche requires further elaboration.

As the most articulate spokesman for life among the authors of the *fin de siècle,* Hofmannsthal carved out more than a niche

1. Jens Malte Fischer, *Fin de siècle* (Munich, 1978), 20–21.
2. See Adrian Del Caro, "Reception and Impact: The First Decade of Nietzsche in Germany," *Orbis Litterarum,* XXXVII (1982), 36, 40, and Fischer, *Fin de siècle,* 15. In this equation, *x* is the human factor that hinders an otherwise perfect equation of nature with art. The Naturalists believed that art and nature are and should be identical.
3. Meyer-Wendt, *Der frühe Hofmannsthal,* 57.

for himself in opposing *not only naturalism* but aestheticism as well. Naturalism and aestheticism are extremes, and Hofmannsthal followed Nietzsche's example in not embracing either cultural movement. In Nietzsche, Hofmannsthal had been impressed by the figure of a man who tolerated life and embraced life precisely because he, Nietzsche, lived on the fringe of society, where lite's waters are keenest, most bracing. Of course Hofmannsthal did not attempt to imitate the hermitlike existence of Nietzsche, nor did he attempt to imitate Nietzsche in any other respect; taking full advantage of his gift, learning, and social station, Hofmannsthal went to work with a heightened awareness of his time and the need to put his time behind him. He was an immediate "insider" of the *fin de siècle*, who cultivated in himself the same kind of broad, historical perspective that enabled Nietzsche to diagnose the ills and identify the currents of his time without wandering aimlessly within the confines of the *Zeitgeist*.

In the poetry of Hofmannsthal, time—as a concept, a dimension, and in every sense as an extension of being—does not much resemble the ontological meditations of Hölderlin and, later on, Heidegger nor the lyrical and existential treatment of time that is so prominent in Nietzsche. I have shown why this is the case by highlighting the other expressions of *movement* in Hofmannsthal; his concentration on articulating movement on the threshold and into the open supersedes historical concepts of time. For Nietzsche, the exploration of the open is achieved, paradoxically and with a distinct existential bent, with the eternal recurrence of the same and a conceptualization of time as infinitely circular, in deliberate contrast to linear time and the associations inherent in linear time conception. For Hofmannsthal, the experience of life takes place within the spectrum of animation, so that time as duration is frequently suspended.

In his most sustained lyrical treatment of historical time, Hofmannsthal revealed his chief concern by entitling the poem "Life" ("Leben"). This concern is stated in lines 1–4:

> The sun sinks upon the lifeless days
> And sinks upon the city, gilding and powerful,
> As once it sank upon the age that had much
> To say and much to give, rich in content.
>
> (*KA*, I, 28)

The criticism of contemporary life implied in the first line serves as the transition to the remote historical past, a time of abundance in which mankind was given much. The setting sun is used as an image of transition in its own right; its setting now, in the present, reminds the poet of how in historical figurative terms it set on the earlier culture. But the image is expanded in the remainder of the first strophe when the ensuing darkness and shadows dissolve the contemporary properties of day, so that "all the hours that glide by, / Are filled with a breath of radiant possibilities."

At this stage the poet-subject is no longer situated in the present but has crossed into the past. A mythological dawn is described, and as the sun rises, "companions find each other / Stepping out of the foliage." Their thoughts, once isolated, now blossom in animated dialogue. The poet speaks for historical humanity by introducing the third strophe with "And now all things become lively for us." With this mythical advent of speech and conviviality, the breath of maenads stirs the trees, and the dryads whisper dreamily of beauty that has passed. On this note of passing, historical time is once again sounded, so that the fourth strophe begins "But we have already stepped out of this garden" (KA, I, 28–29).

Instead of returning his subject to the present, the departure from the mythical garden takes place within the past, and the time travel continues aboard galleys that wait on the golden water. In this historical stage mankind is present, as seen in the sailing of the galleys, and on their approach to the island of their destination the travelers are greeted by the music of flutes until they see

> the chorus moving solemnly,
> To summon Bacchus and the Muses
> Who created tragedy from intoxication.
> (KA, I, 29)

This day of time travel comes to an end, and in the glow of torches and the leaping shadows "Is the tragedy royally concluded." The travelers turn homeward through the night:

> And like the forms that sank into dark
> So too all earthly life concluded
> And like sleep, to the gentle beat of waves,
> Welcomed now would death approach.
> (KA, I, 29)

Similar to the device used in "Experience," the subject of "Life" is aboard a ship from which he is able to view life, but the ship passes by without touching shore.

It would perhaps be unwise to attach profound meaning to "Life," since most of the poem is an allegory treating the journey through life by describing a mythical journey through history. But the nature of history seen in this poem, and the poem's title, point to the idea everywhere visible in Hofmannsthal's poetry that a life must be consummated, and consummation of life requires movement. The Dionysian imagery of the poem first details the earliest historical stage of mankind, when mystical beings introduce speech and mortals celebrate life by observing the animation of all things. The second stage is beyond the mythical garden, when separation between ourselves and nature is symbolized by our journey aboard the galleys. During this stage, the concept of transitoriness is fathomed in the worship of Dionysus, symbol of life and resurrecting life, and the birth of tragedy, as Nietzsche would say, from the spirit of music. Art and consciousness go hand in hand.

Having witnessed the tragedy enacted by the Dionysian chorus, it can be said that the traveler has witnessed life and is prepared for death, because tragedy was the highest gesture of life affirmation among the ancients. It is this understanding that the poet referred to in the first strophe when he maintained that the past had much to offer. Crossing the threshold from present to past can animate our lives in the present, but the poem's conclusion does not seriously address the issue of how the "lifeless days" ("den lebenleeren Tagen") of line 1 are to be animated, because the subject of the poem declares himself ready for death without returning to the historical present.

Hofmannsthal was unequivocal about the value he attached to the past and about the importance of maintaining a vital link with the past. When he addressed himself to man's conception of nature in "Nox Portentis Gravida," he criticized our propensity for regarding nature as the realm of the "eternally cheerful," and the poet was taken to task for his efforts aimed at *dividing* the world so that he can feel more comfortable within it. A vital relation to the past does not idealize nature, and it does not establish a separate, privileged realm for man in the operations of art; art is supposed to engage life, not flee it, and the function of the poet as the articulator of life is to find the voice of things that otherwise remain mute.

The magician of "A Dream of Great Magic" left the subject of the poem so touched that the poet concluded, "And [He] lives in me, as I live in my hand" (*KA*, I, 53). But let us return to the first magical operation of the great magician as he is establishing a dialogue with mortals; when he seats himself, the magician speaks a wondrous "You" to "days that appeared long forgotten to us." As a result of addressing these days with the familiar pronoun (*Du*), they become alive and come forth in all their glory, so that the magician is moved to laughter and tears in his pleasure (*KA*, I, 53). I see this as a metaphor for the kind of relation Hofmannsthal desires between present and past. The past is not inferior to the present when judged by the scale of life, and its "death" is real only insofar as the mentality of the present ascribes greater value to linear progression. The magician is the greatest, most affirmative being in relation to life because he savors life in all its manifestations, past and present. Indeed, a great part of the deadness or unliving of our lives is caught up in our static relation to the past; if the past cannot animate us, we carry it about within us like stones, dead ballast.

A prominent feature of Hofmannsthal's conception of time is its undimensionality. By undimensionality I mean that time does not behave as we are accustomed to perceiving it, so that events do not necessarily occur in succession. The poem "On Transitoriness" ("Über Vergänglichkeit") was written to mark the occasion of the death of Hofmannsthal's close friend, Josephine von Wertheimstein, whose suffering the poet witnessed (*KA*, I, 226–28). And yet, it is not the passing away of a cherished friend and the desire to sustain her memory that animates Hofmannsthal's notion of time, for discernible in his poem are the familiar motifs of gliding and spilling over that characterize his understanding of the open.

What I term "gliding and spilling over" are phenomena abundantly evident in Hofmannsthal's poems, but they are also suggested by George Lukács in *The Theory of the Novel*. Basing his own view of time on Bergson's *durée*, that is, *duration* as "real time," Lukács speaks of duration as that which "advances" to and "passes on" from the instant of memory.[4] The original German is much closer to Hofmannsthal's semantics; "von der zugleitenden und hinweggleitenden Dauer." Hofmannsthal's efforts to depict the undimensionality of time might be seen as the articulation of encounters between lyrical time, based on memory, and time as *durée*, which is also based on memory but is capable of being punctured by lyrical time.

Gliding, like slipping, is a spatial operation and as such is still subject to the abstracting process with which we "tell time" but do not countenance time (*durée*). However, gliding and slipping are both suggestive of breaks in the abstract model of time, because they are operations describing things out of control or, better, out of our con-

4. Georg Lukács, *The Theory of the Novel*, trans. Anna Bostock (Cambridge, Mass., 1971), 126, 121.

trol. Both verbs minimize the utilitarian, time-telling nature of experience and are therefore appropriate poetic expressions capable of
touching the "profound self" that for Bergson is identical with pure
durée.[5]

"On Transitoriness" is one of three *Terzinen* we have already discussed, the others being "The Hours!" and "We are such stuff as
dreams." The poet begins by posing a rhetorical question: How is it
that he can still feel the breath of his friend on his cheek, since those
days are gone forever? The answer lies in the nature of life itself. "This
is a thing," the poet reveals, "that no one fully solves, / And much too
horrifying to lament: / That everything glides and spills and passes
by" (*KA*, I, 45). Apparently stronger than the horror of absolute death
is the unfathomable nature of life, for instead of placing a specific
point of termination on a human life—in this case Hofmannsthal's
friend—life allows for a gliding and blending in spite of death, such
that he can feel (and not only seem to feel) his friend's breath. When
Lukács speaks of "experiences of time which are victories over time,"
and concludes by writing that in these experiences "we come as near
as we can, in a world forsaken by God, to the essence of things," he is
addressing the manner in which the novel or novelist sustains time.[6]
Hofmannsthal's poet also sustains time in the sense of *durée*, as seen
in the epigram "Poets and Present," but the lyrical time of the poet's
work in the poem, as opposed to the poet's relation to community,
triumphs over time in a different sense. For Hofmannsthal the "essence of things" is glimpsed in the immediacy of experience.

The poetic experience or poetic act resembles Bergson's *intuition*,
whereby "one carries oneself into the interior of an object to coincide
with what is unique and therefore inexpressible in it."[7] But "inexpres-
sibility" never prevented a poet from saying what he had to say, and
the poet's best work lies in rescuing for memory those perceptions
whose *accumulation* contributes to real life, real time. Real time is only
possible, according to Bergson, through memory and the accumulated fullness of the past, while our spatial or abstract notion of time
is the artificial, day-to-day abbreviation with which we establish our
bearings.[8] If we accept Bergson's *durée* as authentic time existing con-
currently with authentic living, it is encumbent upon the poet to harvest as much from the past as possible, in order to ensure that *durée* is

5. Leszek Kolakowski, *Bergson* (Oxford, 1985), 17, 19.
6. Lukács, *Theory of the Novel*, 123–24.
7. Kolakowski, *Bergson*, 24.
8. *Ibid.*, 3, 15, 16.

in fact experienced to some extent by otherwise spatially-deflected, and spatially-affected, living.

When the poet serves as chronicler he exercises an authority enabling him to preserve the spatial, abstract dimensions of time. Essentially the poet as chronicler relies more on credibility than on poetic effect; this is why philosophers since Socrates have wrestled with the poets for primacy. However, in poetic practice the poet experiences a contact with *durée* itself, or with what Bergson called the profound self, and the poet may transmit some of this experience by translating it into language and preserving it in memory.

Hofmannsthal's unfathomable "thing" is too horrifying to lament. As prone as we are to lament the passing of a human life, still there is something certain, something final to death. We are able to ritualize the passing of a loved one by expressing grief, through lamentation, because it is our perception that the departed one is truly and irretrievably departed. Not so, says Hofmannsthal, and that is the horror of it: We are not abandoned by the departed, not separated from them by an absolute barrier marking the difference between life and death. The dead live with us, and we with them, however uncomfortable or morbid this may seem. The nature of life and time (*durée*) is not such that we can render it into segments or epochs, let alone detach those segments we deem useless or irretrievable. Indeed, given the all-important function of memory in poetic language, it is precisely the past that animates the present, and relating to the past is the threshold to the open.

The motif of gliding is continued in the third strophe. The poet senses his own self (*Ich*),

> inhibited by nothing,
> Glided over from a small child,
> Strangely mute and foreign as a dog to me.
>
> (*KA*, I, 45)

The self's or ego's ability to glide from a child into the adult subject and to remain somehow foreign to oneself reflects Hofmannsthal's perception of the self as a metaphor, and the disruption of the principle of individuation is a constant theme of the poetry.

To underscore this point, the concluding strophe adds a temporal expansion to the gliding effect:

> Then: that I was a hundred years ago
> And my ancestors, in their shrouds,
> Are related to me like my very own hair.

All of these intuitions or divinings were introduced in the second strophe, when the poet maintained that the phenomenon of the dead lingering among the living is unfathomable and beyond lament. The poet himself has crossed thresholds similar to death, first when his own self (consciousness) glided over to him from a little child and second, when he perceives his ancestors to be intimately a part of him, like his own hair.

The most famous treatment of the ancestor occurs in "Song of Life," where the heir receives the ointment from the hands of the dead old woman. Here too the undimensionality of time is evident, not only because the heir is capable of a physical contact with the ancestor but also because the heir is not burdened by the ancestor's wealth—he squanders it, he celebrates his freedom in the open, finding the threshold of every place (*KA*, I, 63). Conversely, in a linear conception of time, the heir would be determined by the ancestor. First, he could not accept the precious ointment from the ancestor's dead hands, *i.e.*, the ancestor would have to be absolutely dead, and the ointment would have to be accepted at one remove from the dead old woman. This would have the effect of determining the content or "essence" of the ointment, since it would now represent what the old woman carried with her from life into death, that being her "absolute" life (her limited one). The preciousness of the ointment would inhere in the value conferred upon it by the ancestor's *temporal life*.

Second, the heir would be further determined by his ancestor in a linear conception of time because he is expected to *hold* the ointment, save and cherish it, just as it had been saved by the old woman. The saving or preserving of the ointment is a gesture connoting faith in linear time; we succeed in life, ostensibly, when we have some thing—some tenable, precious commodity—that we can pass along to our heirs. If the heir adopts the thing in this same spirit of reverence for what is tenable, he continues to invest linear time with faith and is therefore expected to treat the thing with due reverence, as an heirloom. Preservation of an heirloom keeps alive the link with the past into a linear future—it is succession as humans have practiced it since time immemorial.

Hofmannsthal's heir squanders the ointment on animals, demonstrating, as did the act of dipping into the realm of death to accept it, that he is uninhibited with respect to time. For this same reason— namely, that linear time does not limit him—he is able to smile when life's wrinkles "whisper death" (*KA*, I, 63). The heir's aliveness (*Lebendigkeit*) owes to his skill in confronting the gliding between life and death, just as Hofmannsthal described the phenomenon in "On Transitoriness." The heir is one who is not weighed down by the ballast that death is for most people, even while they are living.

Time's traditional authority to dictate absolute moments of life and death is also questioned in "Good Hour" ("Gute Stunde"). The poem was written in March, 1896, along with "Song of Life" (KA, I, 298), and it contains not only a similar view of time but also the motif of being everywhere at home or, more traditionally, homelessness. The subject of the poem has a titanic perspective; his life is not limited to himself, but resides in all things and in all people, even after his death.

The poem begins with the subject lying, on top of the world, as it seems to him, where he has neither house nor tent. All around him he perceives the roads of men—those leading up to the mountains and those leading down to the sea. Traveling these roads are people: "They carry the wares, that they enjoy, / Unknowing that each contains my life" (KA, I, 64). In their woven baskets they carry

> The fruits I've not eaten since long ago:
> I recognize the fig, now I sense the place,
> Yet the long forgotten one lives on!
>   (KA, I, 64)

The subject is able to sense the place of origin of the figs because he was there; his life was in the figs, and his life will be consumed by the living and therefore sustain them, even though he has long since been forgotten in time.

Time is stripped of its ultimate authority in the final strophe: "And when life, the beautiful, was taken from me, / It endured in the sea and endured in the land!" It is puzzling to reflect on the title of this poem, since defiance of time is at stake here, but the suggestive title prepares the reader for an unorthodox treatment of time. The expression "good hour" is equivocal in German in very much the same way it is in English. One reading is to interpret the "good" as a value; if hours can be good, which is to say, if the measuring of time has value, then a "good hour" would look like this (and defy everything we have come to expect from an hour). "Good hour" can also be used to indicate a full hour, as in the phrase "He left here a good hour ago." Another idiomatic usage might suggest something like "in good time" (zur guten Stunde).

"Good Hour" can also reflect on the precise time of the subject's experience, which is an experience beyond the threshold of linear time enabling him to feel his kinship with the living, the dead, and all places past and present. This phenomenon was described in "The Hours!" with a similar gliding of life into death as the subject stared out at the bluing sea, and in this poem too the word "hour" in the title has to be taken not as an absolute measure of absolute time but as a metaphor.

The heir of "Song of Life" lives with the potential and promise of his ancestors, but not in such a way that he feels constrained. There is a sovereignty in the heir that he could not demonstrate if he allowed time to be sovereign over him. Hofmannsthal gave this idea elaborate expression in "The Emperor of China Speaks:" ("Der Kaiser von China spricht:"). The emperor is literally a sovereign, but what must have guided Hofmannsthal in his choice of subject, as Freny Mistry has argued compellingly, is the author's "own distinct conviction of ancestral significance and life beyond the grave."[9]

From the outset the emperor's presence, his living in the here and now, is perceived by him as both the center of the universe and the most important point in time: "In the midst of all things / Dwell I the son of heaven" (KA, I, 72). The specification of his place as the perfect center and the words "Dwell I" are the most affirmative expression possible; throughout the poem the pronouns "my" or "mine" are repeated thirteen times. But these possessive pronouns are misleading if they are construed as emanating from a monstrous ego, a figure intoxicated by himself, and we have come to expect from Hofmannsthal that such an ego does not exist.

A motif of the poem is the emperor's relation to the walls that exist within his kingdom. Lines 3–10 delimit what is closest to the emperor:

> My women, my trees,
> My animals, my ponds
> Are enclosed by the first wall.
> Below lie my ancestors:
> Entombed with their weapons,
> Their crowns on their heads,
> As befits each of them,
> They dwell in the vaults.
>
> (KA, I, 72)

Despite the radically affirmative "me" and "now" of the first two lines, the emperor is in fact very much other-oriented by the exten-

9. Freny Mistry, "Hofmannsthal's 'Der Kaiser von China spricht,' " *Modern Language Review*, LXXI (1976), 68.

sions of himself—namely, his women, plants, animals, and ponds, which lie within the borders of the first wall. These people and things are held close to him by virtue of lying within the borders of the first wall; they are his link to the expanded present. What is more, even the earth beneath the denizens of the present lays its claim on the sovereign: His ancestors are appropriately arrayed in their tombs below, where they are said to dwell. The ancestors are the sovereign's link to the past, and as Mistry points out, "The whole of Chinese religion and social life revolved around the worship of parents and ancestors."[10]

In expanding, concentric circles the emperor goes on to describe himself in relation to the world. His majesty, he maintains, resounds deep into the bowels of the earth, and at his feet originate rivers flowing in all four directions, "To water my garden, / Which is the wide earth." In the waters of these rivers are reflected the emperor's animals, colorful cities, dark walls, dense forests, "And faces of many peoples." The rivers themselves serve as a sort of second wall, because they reflect and in that way contain what is within them.

The emperor next returns to describe in greater detail the people who are nearest to him. Lines 24–33 detail how his nobles, like the stars, dwell around him, bearing names he has given them, with women he has given them, and they are surrounded by their numerous children:

> For all the nobles of this earth
> I created eyes, carriage and lips,
> As the gardener with his flowers.
> (KA, I, 72)

Once again, the emperor's egocentricity seems boundless, and in a sense perhaps it is, but at the same time, he expresses his radical sovereignty by detailing the subjects—nobles, wives, and children—who stand in the same relation to him as the flowers to the gardener. The analogy of the gardener should be pursued: Someone who admires or remarks upon the flowers in a particular garden does not normally associate the beauty or lushness of the flowers with the perceived or alleged arrogance of the gardener. On the contrary, if anything is attributed to the gardener, it is more likely to be by way of praise for the skill and care in nurturing such beautiful plants.

10. *Ibid.*

The final lines once again take up the theme of expansion, and describe, not the people closest to the sovereign, but those who are furthest removed.

> But between outer walls
> Dwell peoples my warriors,
> Peoples my plowmen.
> New walls and then again
> Those subjugated peoples,
> Peoples of ever duller blood
> Unto the sea, the last wall,
> Which encircles my empire and me.
>
> (*KA*, I, 73)

The outer wall encloses the multitudes of the emperor, those who are not nobles but nonetheless within his keeping, for they are described with the pronoun "my." Beyond these multitudes lie the subjugated peoples whose blood is said to be "ever duller" ("immer dumpfern Blutes"); their relation to the sovereign is tenuous, their spirit inscrutable to him because they do not belong, by choice, to the sovereign. Their physical distance from the sovereign is commensurate with their spiritual distance from him; he is not responsible for them in the same way that he nurtures the others.

Beyond the wild, subjugated peoples the sovereign's empire is walled in by the sea, and he recognizes the sea as the last wall enclosing not only his empire but himself as well. The sovereign, that is to say, reaches his limit where his empire reaches its limit. It is significant that near the center of all things—closest to the emperor himself—are his nobles, whom he has cultivated like a garden, and his ancestors, dwelling in the earth. They are all within the first circle, and the ancestors nourish him even as he gives nourishment and form to the nobles. In contrast to this intimacy, this giving and nurturing of form, the outermost wall of the empire is formless: it is the sea, and it contains as its nearest dwellers those peoples most hostile to the emperor—the subjugated. Because they are subjugated, these peoples will not adopt the form imparted by the emperor.

The entire poem of forty-one lines is related in first-person, present tense. When there is mention of the past, as with respect to the ancestors and the emperor's descriptions in lines 26–32 of how he gave characteristics to his nobles, the implication is not of a stronger or better historical past but merely a grammatical tense that flows easily, smoothly into the present and dwells there as if there were no other moment but the present. At the same time, the emperor's words suggest that things have always been this way and always will be, because the walls lie where they should, and within the walls lie those who should be situated there. Time is once again divested by Hofmannsthal of its dimensionality. Here the emperor, not time, is sovereign, and the emperor's sovereignty has everything to do with living in a proper balance with other living things, ancestors included, so that time is hardly a factor and the emperor's speaking seems to create an infinite present.

The abundant present resulting from the emperor's undimensional relation to time characterizes the primacy of life over time. Judged by the standard of abstract time, the emperor's sovereignty exists only lyrically, since in chronological terms he must fade into oblivion like everyone else. However, insofar as the poet is here to suspend time and, in effect, serve as the guarantor of *durée* as opposed to the teller of time, the celebration of the emperor in the poem serves mnemonically to rescue him and his living. The establishment of *durée* through memory is the oldest and most noble work of the poet, so that Hölderlin too devoted much of his ontology to memory.[11]

In the poem "Message" Hofmannsthal described his exploration of the landscape of the soul that united him and his friend beyond temporal and spatial dimensions; he invited the friend to drink with him "from those pitchers that are my inheritance" and to celebrate friendship as a common wandering in landscapes transformed into a "realm of soul" by conviviality and dialogue (*KA*, I, 78). Within the same time frame, August to September of 1897, "Verses to a Little Child" ("Verse auf ein kleines Kind") was written, and once again the motif of friendship inspired Hofmannsthal to test the bonds of abstract time.

"Verses" was written to celebrate the birth of Richard Beer-Hofmann's daughter, Miriam, and in a letter to his close friend, Hofmannsthal pledged that he would be a good friend to the child in years to come (*KA*, I, 341). The poem has a prayerlike quality, insofar as it is addressed to the baby as a promise and prophecy of what lies in store for her, as if Hofmannsthal were attempting to clear a path for the child into the world that he knew himself was open:

> Your rosy feet are growing
> To seek the lands of sun:
> The lands of sun are open!
> (*KA*, I, 79)

11. See Del Caro, *Hölderlin*, 42–47, 92–98.

The child will grow and learn to walk, and the child's walking should take her into the open, into lands of sun. Here, the poet continued, the air of millennia still hangs in the trees, and the inexhaustible seas are still there.

Hofmannsthal employed a fairy-tale image of the child who shares its milk with a toad and is rewarded with riches, and of a friendly dolphin that will come to shore and be her companion.[12] Should the dolphin sometimes not come, "Then the eternal winds / Will soon still your flowing tears." The poet assures the child that in the lands of sun "The old, illustrious times" are still there, and there forever. In conclusion:

> The sun with secret power,
> It forms your rosy feet
> To walk its eternal land.
> (*KA*, I, 79)

The time factor in the poem begins with the physical growth of the child, whose limbs have yet to grow. By the time the child begins to walk, before two years, she will be ready to step into the open where time is measured in thousands of years, and where the seas are inexhaustible. Hofmannsthal uses land, sea, sun, wind, fairy tale, and saga to connect generations in a bond that stretches time, in a place designated as the eternal open.

A strange twist of time occurs in a late poem Hofmannsthal wrote about the end of life, as opposed to the promise of beginning life in "Verses." "The Old Man's Longing for the Summer" ("Des alten Mannes Sehnsucht nach dem Sommer"), written about 1905, is a sobering treatment of transitoriness, disguised with motifs of romanticism à la Eichendorff but intensified by a mood of transience very similar to Hermann Hesse's "Vergänglichkeit." The poem is written in three-line strophes, with the first and third lines rhyming, except for the beginning and end of the poem, which are accorded only one line. As the title indicates, an old man is expressing longing for summer. The problem of time is immediately apparent in the first line: "If only it were July instead of March" (*KA*, I, 104).

Allegorically speaking, and in keeping with a linear view of time, the old man would not be longing for July, representing summer, but for an earlier season, for the incipient life of youth connoted by spring. But the old man finds himself in March, wishing for July, even

---

12. For sources in Grimm and Oesterly see *KA*, I, 343.

though he will be older in July (literally and figuratively). Using this device, Hofmannsthal stresses at the outset of his poem that the old man's nostalgia is not for youth, but for summer, *i.e.*, for the fullest, most abundant episode of life. The old man does not want the beginning; he wants it all.

As he begins to steep himself in his reverie, or his fantasy, the old man thinks in subjunctive terms. In lines 1–16 he dreams of how things would be; with nothing to hinder him, he would take a trip across country where large groups of trees would stand, and he remarks inwardly, "How long it's been since I've seen their like!" He would climb down from his horse or hail the coachman and travel without destination forward "into the summer land's depths." And beneath such trees he would rest, and in their branches would be day and night at the same time "and not like in this house." The approach of a time in which night and day are equal, without one crowding the other, suggests a transition to a timeless state. Once again the subjunctive is clouded by the old man's momentary return to present time and his present gloom. For in his house it is only bleak:

> Where days sometimes are drear as night
> And nights barren and lurking like the day,
> There everything would be life, gleam and splendor.

At this point the old man seems to have control over his fantasy, and his experience is recounted in present tense.

He steps from "the shadow" into the joyous evening light, feels a breeze, but nowhere does he hear whispered "All this is nothing." In the darkening valley he sees the lights of houses, and though the darkness blows over him, the night wind does not speak of dying. He walks across the cemetery and sees only flowers bowing in the faint light; "Of nothing else at all do I feel a nearness." And between the hazel bushes that are growing dark, water is flowing. Like a child he listens and does not hear whispered "This is all in vain." The old man undresses and jumps into the water, and when he lifts his head the moon is high as he splashes about in the brook. He raises himself halfway from the ice-cold water, and standing now in the bright moonlight, he tosses a flat stone far out into the land. The old man's experience of summer ends here, for the last three strophes depart from his first-person perspective and are given in omniscient third person (*KA*, I, 105).

But there is a triumph of living expressed in lines 17–34, from the point when the old man steps out of the shadow to when he stands naked in the moonlight and throws the stone. Having literally stepped out of shadow, the old man is no longer under the sway of time, no longer governed in his thinking by thoughts of transitoriness—he has liberated himself from the vacillating subjunctive and the death associations that held him there. In this new life, this life of the summer land, the old man does not allow himself to be shortchanged by the ballast of death in life. His experiences are untainted and become increasingly free of death, a progression that Hofmannsthal illustrates in four strophes by stressing the man's consciousness of having overcome death, then removing death from the field entirely in the two strophes that conclude the old man's experience. His bathing in the brook and his emerging from the brook to throw a stone into the darkness are actions completely untouched by reflection, so that no mention of death accompanies them.

The shadow returns:

> And on the moonlit summer land
> Falls a wide shadow: is it he who sadly
> Nods here, here behind the pillow on the wall?
> (KA, I, 105)

The poet-narrator enters the summer night concurrent with the falling shadow, dissolving the image of the youthful phantom left standing in the moonlight. The old man is identified with the shadow, with death, because he has returned to his former condition of life with death:

> So glum and sad, who cowers half upright
> Before day and stares grimly into twilight
> And knows that something lurks for both of us?
>
> He, who in this March is so tortured
> By the evil wind that he never lies down nights
> And cramps his black hands over his heart?
>
> Oh where is July and the summer land!
> (KA, I, 105)

It is the poet's lament we hear in the last line, not the old man's, but the old man had started the meditation. Once he has exhausted the last bit of life by sojourning briefly in the summer land, the old man is spent. His reprieve was courageous, if not substantial; the second time around he knew how to live. But standing in the bright moonlight as the transfigured old man, after having emerged from his symbolic cleansing in the stream, the old man must once again cast a shadow, if not literally as a moon shadow then perhaps as the return to his accustomed darkness upon the consummation of his second life. There is no eternal life—at least, not for the individual.

The poet asserts his empathy for the old man who can do nothing now but await death, and in a way, he spells him and takes the vigil onto himself. By taking upon himself the suffering and longing of the old man, the poet's final lament is an exclamation of how keenly he himself has experienced the unclouded life, the open life. This empathy is demonstrated by the wording of the poet's lament; instead of uttering a wish in the subjunctive mood, as the old man did, the poet specifically asks "where is July and the summer land!" He has adopted the old man's longing based on the old man's experience of the summer land.

July is of course a time, while the summer land, apparently, is a place. Even if both expressions are a metaphor for life, there is still a conflation of time and place because the open in which life takes place must be an open not only in spatial terms, enabling movement, but also in temporal terms, so that actions are uninhibited, like the old man's. To cry out for July and the summer land as if they were one and the same, or of equal value, is therefore appropriate, since the experience of open life will elude us if we persist in crippling life with the "medusa gaze" that sees death and futility in all things, in all actions. When the Time monolith that we all harbor within us is broken down, the greatest weight of time—awareness of death—suddenly begins to lighten. As in the case of the old man, the emphasis shifts from reflection and regret to uninhibited actions resulting in consummated life. When time and place become one, there is life.

What I have designated as the undimensionality of time is basically Hofmannsthal's attempt to attack the Time monolith. There is no doubt that an unhealthy, subservient relation to time detracts significantly from the experience of life. Let us imagine, for the purpose of clarification, that the Time monolith is a huge bell tower. Wherever we wander, whatever we undertake, the shadow of this tower darkens our path. And if we seem to adjust to the dimming light and find life in the shadow not so bad after all, our compromised peace of mind is shattered every hour and half hour by the tolling of the bell in the tower—its sound penetrates any distance and jerks us back to the center, which is the tower.

Therefore a number of Hofmannsthal's poems were dedicated to breaking down the monolith, so that, once free of the thralldom in its shadow, the open life can be explored without interference. Still another effective device Hofmannsthal used to "soften" time is time compression. Instead of breaking up and breaking down formidable periods, spans, lengths of time, lifetimes, etc., the poet takes otherwise formidable segments of time and compresses them into moments of experience. In my discussion of preexistence the point was made and underscored that for Hofmannsthal, a life does not necessarily manifest itself simply because a human form assumes its quantum of space and inhales its quantum of air for a set number of years. By the same reasoning, it is dangerous to equate life with the passage of so-and-so many years, and unfair to deny the possibility of life where only brief intervals are at stake.

Time compression accurately describes what takes place in the poem "Infinite Time" ("Unendliche Zeit"). In this short poem of ten lines, without rhyme or meter, the emphasis is on the collapsing of infinite time into a moment; reflected in the style of the poem is the openness demanded by its subject. The poet addresses his friend about an event from the past: "Really, are you too weak to remember that blissful time?" (*KA*, I, 51). The special time of which the poet speaks is then described, using the narrative past. The stars emerged above the darkening valley, but the friends stood in shadow and shivered. The giant elm shook itself as if in dream, showering drops all around them into the grass:

> Not an hour had passed
> Since that rain! And to me it seemed infinite time.
> For life expands for one who experiences, without sound
> Chasms of infinite dream open up between two glances:
> I had absorbed your twenty-year existence into me
> —So it seemed, even as the tree still held its drops.
>
> (*KA*, I, 51)

It is unlikely that the friend participated in this experience, since unlike "Message" there is no real dialogue here, only the rhetorical question used to trigger the remembering of a blissful moment. The friend is not so much weak as he is incapable of compressing time within his own being. He would not have a recollection of this moment beyond the traditional references of space and time.

The friends had been standing for scarcely an hour beneath the great tree, sheltering themselves from the rainstorm. But the poet does not begin at the starting point of this experience; instead, he begins with the emergence of the stars *after* the rain, as the friends shiver in the cool, night air. This is a skillful transition from the infinite time experience, because that experience glides easily into the starry sky, but less easily into the dark earth. Still, when the subject gets around to measuring the experience on a temporal scale, he realizes, to his acute surprise, that it had lasted barely an hour. During the rainstorm he had been somewhere else—his life was not identical with his ego—and the washing, rinsing qualities of an evening rain shower provide the perfect medium for the diffusion of self that occurs here.

An explanation is provided for why the hour became infinite time or, let us say, for why the subject ceased to be a subject subject to time. Literally the line is translated "*to* the experiencing one life expands" ("dem Erlebenden dehnt sich das Leben"). In German the verb "to live" (*leben*) is itself expanded into the verb "to experience" (*erleben*), adding a natural propensity to equate living with experiencing. The noun "life" is a verbative noun transforming *leben* to *Leben* (*das Leben*). The phrase "to the experiencing one" therefore contains the meaning "to the one who is living" or to the one who is engaged in the operation of living. The act or operation of living, freed from temporal associations, opens chasms of infinite dream that are experienced in the temporal span of mere glances. Since the experiencing of life in the expansion of life is not measurable, the poet resorts to metaphor; chasms of infinite dream fill and animate the space that time cannot.

Hofmannsthal was quite serious about this view of experience in the compression of time, as witnessed in a detailed letter to his father of July 13, 1895. He explained that he was driven by a powerful desire to apprehend or gain mastery of the present. The practice of art, in his view, was nothing more than a striving to multiply the present by assimilating strange life and totally living out (*ausleben*) one's own presence through reflection, and recalling the vanished present:

> Since time is something highly relative, a mere form of mental perception, one can actually place infinite content into a moment, and I am firmly convinced that in fact I sometimes experience more on a ride with the tramway than another person on a journey. I can imagine that one could dispense with the concept of fleeing time almost as easily as the concept of the insignificant, and this lies in the remarkable phrase: il faut glisser la vie, ne pas l'appuyer. In art this ideal balance is actually produced: there is in art nothing insignificant (so too in dreams) and in all their flux, appearances still have eternal duration as ideas. (*KA*, I, 249)

The operative phrase here is "we must let life glide," which Hofmannsthal adopted from the French. The thoughts he revealed to his father are in keeping with the broader poetic in which Hofmannsthal attempted to explore the open life; as a relative concept in itself, a "mere form of mental perception," time must not be allowed to constrain the living by imposing barriers and judgments everywhere. That operation of judgmental time was seen in "The Old Man" when he had to wrest life from the judgments of passing, of transitoriness that shadowed his experiences. Bergson referred to the condition of being constrained within a body subject to laws of matter as the "superficial self."[13] But I do not mean to personify time as the evil, insidious agent of life obstruction—*we mortals* are not time but life, and when life has ascendancy over time, things are in their proper order and we have time for living.

I see this proper relation between time and life reflected in the epigram "Poets and Present," already discussed at some length. The poet senses that something is amiss with time, and he addresses it as "confused time." He is quite aware that he holds time suspended above the chaos into which it will fall without his solicitude. Time's response to the poet, who laments the fact that he must serve both as time's wings and as its supporter or rescuer, can now be seen in the light of time compression. Time tells the poet to take comfort; things have always been so, and if this state causes the poet to be in awe and tremble, all the better—*living is manifest* in the shuddering ones, in the poets who are chosen ones, and because of the ascendancy of life manifest in the poet, the poets must sustain time. It should be noted that as long as the poet serves as time's wings, he, the poet, takes it where he wants.

As a final example of time compression I offer "Before Day" ("Vor Tag"), a poem written in 1907 and perhaps the last truly formidable published poem, in the sense that it illustrates major tenets of Hofmannsthal's poetic. The poem of thirty-nine lines in free verse details the events of a few moments before dawn. In conception the poem reminds one of Mörike's "On a Winter Morning, Before Sunrise," but Hofmannsthal's extremely dense, animated weave of figures and images points back to his own rich lyrical work of the 1890s.

The word "now" occurs ten times; it opens the poem and is featured in both terse sentences of the poem's last line. The events of the poem are compressed into the moment; all the figures are in their appropriate place and time without necessarily following one another in succession. The "now" device is used to give each event its *pro-*

13. Kolakowski, *Bergson*, 17.

prium, and Hofmannsthal avoids time adverbs like "then" in his effort
to dispel the Time monolith ("then" is used once). Present tense is
used throughout.

On the washed-out horizon, collapsed upon itself, lies a thunder-
storm in its last throes. Now a sick person lying in bed thinks to himself; " 'Day! now I will sleep!' " (*KA,* I, 106). As the tired man closes
his eyes, a calf in its stall stretches its nostrils to drink in the morning
air. In the silent wood an unwashed hobo stirs from sleep, reaches for
a rock and tosses it at a dove that flies away drunk with sleep; the
hobo shudders as he hears the rock impact heavily with the earth.
This series of images encompassing lines 1–12 is expressed matter-of-
factly—only the actions are described.

Halfway through line 12 the poet's presence begins to be felt more
strongly:

> Now the water runs
> As if it wanted to plunge after the night that
> Crept away, into darkness, unsympathetic, wild
> And in cold mist, while above
> The Savior and the mother softly softly
> Converse upon the little bridge: softly,
> And yet their tiny speech is eternal
> And indestructible like the stars above.
> He bears his cross and says only: "My mother!"
> And looks at her, and "Oh my dear son!"
> Says she. —
>
> (*KA,* I, 106)

Relations are established by the poet in lines 12–22. The running
water of the stream seems to hasten after the vanishing night, and its
effect is described by the poet as unsympathetic (*unteilnehmend*) or
detached, merely wild. But this thin relation, or rather, this relation
imagined by the poet, is superseded by the real relation in what happens above, on the little bridge (a concrete image) standing above the
indifferent water (an ephemeral image). The Savior and his mother
are involved in an eternal dialogue that takes place at this moment,
and they are also involved in an eternal action, like a drama: He *carries*
his cross, speaks, and looks at her; she responds.

This event continuing into present time is animated each time a
person crosses that bridge, looks at the image, and reads the inscription. The dialogue that compresses time into the present, while pulling it out of the remote past that does not die, takes place not only
between the Madonna and the Savior but between their reality and

the reality of the passersby; all walkers who cross this point are reminded of the suffering of Christ and the gift of eternal life.

A different dialogue begins midway through line 22, again pointing to Hofmannsthal's device of keeping all things and events in the
poem close together, related, without established causal or temporal
relations between them.

> Now the heavens and the earth
> Engage in mute oppressive dialogue. Then a
> Shudder passes through the ancient heavy body:
> She musters herself to live the new day.
> Now the ghostly twilight rises.
>
> (KA, I, 106)

Without words the sky and earth engage in an oppressive dialogue,
because the transition from night (sky) to day (earth: feminine *die
Erde*) marks the ascendancy of one over the other. Earth shudders, as
though reluctant to rouse itself, but the rising of dawn's light marks
the transition.

The treatment of the events concentrated in lines 1–26 is for the
most part detached and descriptive. There is no commentary, no
judgment, only the slight intrusion of the poet's omniscience into the
dialogue nexus of lines 16–26. The rest of the poem, moving toward
day, details the actions of a single man. From the distant, dying storm
on the horizon through a series (not a succession) of increasingly
closer, more intimate images, the poet prepares his reader for the last
event before day by introducing a figure with whom one can identify.
If what has occurred up to this point has taken place outside the
bounds of society—including the hobo's actions, since he is outside
of society—then a merging of social and natural will now signal the
advent of time.

The last episode, appropriately enough for this poem, also begins
with the word "now" and breaks up line 26. A barefoot man is creep-
ing away from a woman's bed; running like a shadow and climbing
like a thief, he enters his own room through the window and looks at
himself in the mirror and suddenly he is afraid

> Of this pale overnightish stranger,
> As if he himself on this night
> Had murdered the good boy that he was
> And now returned to wash his hands
> In the pitcher of his victim, as if mockingly,
> And therefore the sky seemed so oppressive

> And everything in the air so unusual.
> Now the stall door creeks. And now is also day.
>   (*KA*, I, 106–07)

The man whose innocence was lost in the night, in the timeless realm where all things have their place and nothing is judged, finds himself transformed when he looks into the mirror. We are familiar with Hofmannsthal's conception of self and the transformation of the self that occurs in the poem "Transformation," and in that poem too the significance of the transformation depends on how we perceive time. The man of "Before Day" sees a "pale overnightish stranger" ("blassen übernächtigen Fremden"); though he finds himself poised to enter the day, his actions from the night still mark him.

In an as-if clause, Hofmannsthal has his transformed man return as a doppelgänger. The doppelgänger is created by the "good boy's" conscience, his past history under the auspices of time (day). Together the former boy and his sense of guilt, the baggage of the night's adventure, create an image in which a strange man (the intensified boy, the boy who is experiencing time compression) washes his hands of the boy's blood. Just as the brook seems to chase the night and effects a mood of detachment as it flows beneath the bridge, so too the water of the man's washing relates back to night, which he tries to "wash his hands" of. In Matthew 27:24–25, "When Pilate saw that he was getting nowhere, but that instead a riot was brewing, he took water and washed his hands over against the crowd, saying, 'I am innocent of this good man's blood; it is your concern.'" I am not arguing here for the man as a Christ figure. However, he is part of the living history and present subsumed in the figure of Christ and the Madonna as they exist not only on the bridge but "in time" as it subsumes mortals. Christ, who died for our sins and stands *above the water*, is a metaphor for continued life, even "eternal life" in the Christian sense, and precisely because of his newly incurred guilt, the man will live.

It is not literally the case that a boy journeyed into the night and returned a man, and therefore was a stranger to himself, for we have to assume that if a man returns at dawn, a man set forth at night. What makes the dawn experience of the man so disturbing, however, is the enormous time compression that occurred during the night; all that living, all that experiencing does, in fact, alter him, but not as time alters one's features and makes a person mindful of intervening years. This alteration is felt, intuited, as a lethargic anxiety attaching to the night's deed. It is guilt.

In this anxious state of mind, sensing the disparity between his earlier self and the guilt-ridden self, the man has an anticipation of a transformed life. Even if his features have not literally transformed, still he sensed the oppressiveness of this particular dawn and is unable to ignore its message. With the ultimate arrival of day, the man must be prepared, even as the earth had to be prepared, to rouse himself, gird himself for the drama that unfolds. For the man who has incurred guilt by virtue of his deed, and has thereby also penetrated from the unliving realm of preexistence into higher life, the drama awaiting him is every bit as disturbing as the frightful stranger who will accompany him from this moment on, and also every bit as sweet as the night he savored on his journey into life.

8 INSCRIPTION

In his book from 1905, Adalbert von Hanstein wrote about 1889 and the decade that followed, explaining that a major concern of this period had been the individual. Talk began to focus on polarities such as the strong versus the weak, the master versus the herd; naturalism's fixation with social issues gave way to explorations of individualism.[1] There is no longer any doubt that Nietzsche's influence on the culture of the *fin de siècle* can be traced to his spirited and eloquent defense of the individual and individualism. Even greatness, as the assertion of a powerful will exerted by an individual, enabling the individual to flourish within and despite his age, was a concept that Nietzsche feared was on the verge of extinction. The values of the West, steeped in Platonism and Christianity and milled in the machinery of democratic institutions since the eighteenth century, were rapidly in decline. Nietzsche relentlessly drew attention to the questions of values: How would the modern person pursue individualism? What goes into the making of an individual in a time of herd values? How do our institutions stand up to the scrutiny of the highest judge of all—life itself?

When Nietzsche's discourse is animated by the enthusiasm for great individuals, the most prominent figures of the modern age are Napoleon, Goethe, and Wagner. All three wielded enormous *influence* and inscribed themselves indelibly in the course of human events—they were all very much alive, and for Nietzsche, great lives manifest themselves in ways that draw events along in a slipstream. Wagner's greatness, as I have argued in *Nietzsche contra Nietzsche*, inspired Nietzsche to assert his own brand of individualism. Wagner was great by popular and esoteric estimations, but the problem with Wagner, Nietzsche argued, was that he was a carrier of decadent values without knowing or caring about it, while he, Nietzsche, made it his task to point to a new set of values in-

1. Adalbert von Hanstein, *Das jüngste Deutschland* (Leipzig, 1905), 191.

tended to halt the slide of mankind toward becoming a species of diminutive, self-effacing creatures. Nietzsche's greatness and influence beside figures like Napoleon, Goethe, and Wagner was etched into history by virtue of the spirited campaign he launched in his search for the values of life.

What did the great individual look like by Hofmannsthal's time? By then Nietzsche was scarcely a contemporary, since he went insane in 1889 and died in 1900, but the truly insightful individuals of the 1890s understood that Nietzsche had been onto something. Hofmannsthal's perceptions of individual greatness were substantially informed by Nietzsche's criteria of life affirmation, and this is reflected in the words of "In Memory of the Actor Mitterwurzer" ("Zum Gedächtnis des Schauspielers Mitterwurzer"), written in 1898. I am not implying that Mitterwurzer was a "great" man on a par with Goethe. The actor's greatness was praised by Hofmannsthal according to values championed by Nietzsche. Hamburger considered this poem important enough to include in his edition of the poems.[2] A sample from this text of sixty-seven lines will suffice to demonstrate the nature of Hofmannsthal's high regard for the actor:

> For in him was something that unlocked many
> Doors and traversed many spaces:
> The power of life, this was in him.
> And over him death gained power!
> Extinguished the eyes whose inner core
> Was covered by secret signs,
> Choked in his throat the thousand voices
> And killed the body which, limb for limb,
> Was laden with lives yet unborn.
>
> (*KA*, I, 83)

The figure of the actor can be seen as a metaphor of transition; we expect the actor to "unlock many doors" by virtue of his gift for entering many roles, and his "thousand voices" express the same capacity to come and go at will. Death killed the body, the poet maintains, and there were many lives within that body, not just the subjective life that perishes with the illusion of the solitary ego.

The secrets inhering in the actor's core were life's secrets, and apparently Mitterwurzer possessed these secrets in abundance, so that he was able to bring life to his roles, bring his roles to life. Hofmannsthal stresses the liberating quality of the actor's work; doors are

2. Hamburger, ed., *Hofmannsthal*.

unlocked and spaces are traversed, so that in every respect the actor was one who encouraged and aided the exploration of the open.

It is this very spirit of encouraging approach to the open life that animates Hofmannsthal's poetry. Hans Steffen, in trying to define precisely where Hofmannsthal stood in relation to Nietzsche, writes that the poet was not concerned with being Nietzsche's successor or exegist but instead was engaged in coming to terms (*Auseinandersetzung*) with the philosopher: "In contrast to his doctrine of the primacy of life, [Hofmannsthal] was concerned with saving the dignity of the uprooted spirit."[3] I can agree with Steffen on each point except one—namely, that Hofmannsthal was somehow opposed to Nietzsche's doctrine of the primacy of life.

Hofmannsthal was clearly *not* opposed to this "doctrine" or he would not have expended so much poetic energy on exploring the language of life. It is certainly fair to say that Hofmannsthal endeavored to preserve the dignity of spirit in an age when art and thought seemed cut adrift from their traditional moorings, but it does not follow that this undertaking is in any way opposed to the primacy of life. The dignity or implied "home" of the spirit that Steffen alludes to is to be found, according to Hofmannsthal, in the open, and the open is finally accessible because the spirit has broken free to explore the open in an authentic, vital relation to living.

This crucial point on the nature of Hofmannsthal's work, as it is linked to the issue of the difference between Nietzsche the philosopher and Hofmannsthal the poet, concerns me very much. I favor the perspective of Hermann Broch, who explained that in the latter part of the nineteenth century, only Nietzsche defied the provincialism of German writing, but he too fell victim to the malaise he himself decried *because he refused to engage art.* "For he, despite the strongest artistic temperament, kept himself aloof of all artistry and poetry. Aside from the few very important but purely furtive poems, Nietzsche considered himself to be an exclusively rational thinker and therefore totally joined ranks with the new position of the German spirit."[4] Broch may be guilty of some overstatement, since Nietzsche clearly did not succeed in expunging the poet from his being, any more than he succeeded totally in disavowing the romantic in him. What is relevant now is the basically accurate insight that Nietzsche willfully chose to champion reason above art. Dangerous as this dichotomy of reason

3. Steffen, "Schopenhauer, Nietzsche, und die Dichtung Hofmannsthals," 74.
4. Broch, *Hofmannsthal und seine Zeit*, 31.

versus art may be to uphold, it is still a useful metaphor for understanding why, in my perception, Hofmannsthal begins where Nietzsche leaves off.

My question is, Can a person speak for life? By speaking for life, I do not limit myself to speaking "in favor" of life—that would be a small virtue indeed. The living generally do not advocate their lives, because the assumption is that wherever there is a pulse, there is life. But Nietzsche often, if not without occasional irony, referred to himself as the spokesman of life (*der Fürsprecher des Lebens*). By attaching himself to life as its spokesman, he wanted to tap the living source, present himself as a medium and example, and in so doing effect an instrumentality between abstract Life and individual. In his writings Nietzsche wanted to win people over to life, to the values of life and the perspectives that affirm it. On this score his writings are persuasive and at times impassioned.

Hofmannsthal, on the other hand, was not a philosopher of Nietzsche's stature—he was not a philosopher in the historical sense that Nietzsche embraced. Even if we grant validity to Nietzsche's claim that he dispensed with traditional philosophy in favor of adopting the philosophy of life, still it is apparent that he embarked on his new philosophizing very much aware of the historical baggage of philosophy. That is, even as the "new philosopher" and free spirit, Nietzsche spoke in philosophical terms *for life*. Hofmannsthal's discourse of the 1890s does not champion life as a cause, philosophical or otherwise—rather, it speaks with and out of life. While Nietzsche constantly tried to draw on his experiences in living to provide a vitalistic basis to his thought, he was compelled to retreat to the rational medium of philosophical discourse to explain himself, to be sufficiently persuasive.

Hofmannsthal's poetry does not bear the marks of this tension arising between living and writing about life. Hofmannsthal's inscription in life is an action undertaken for the sake of living, and his poems, not subjected to the same scrutiny as philosophical discourse, remain a more authentic articulation of life than writing about life. Speaking as he does with and out of life, his danger more closely resembles the experience of Chandos. Chandos eschews the discourse of his community because he, too, keenly feels the discourse of life beyond the threshold of self, and he has no incentive, feels no lasting compunction to return to community in order to provide a record of his experiences (Nietzsche's task). Essentially, Hofmannsthal-Chandos is not concerned with winning others over to his position; he has more than enough on his plate with the language that throws him before the unspeakable *presence* and present that life is.

This idea was formulated with exceptional clarity in Hofmannsthal's one-page essay "Poets and Life": "Knowledge about representability [*Darstellbarkeit*] consoles us against being overwhelmed by life; knowledge about life consoles us against the shadowyness of portrayal." This intimate relationship, moreover, tends to pull down a weak talent, but it impels the strong talent upward (*Prosa I*, 287). Ultimately, then, it is Hofmannsthal's view that a writer must affirm the symbiotic relationship between art (representation) and life and the strong writer will be uplifted. This resembles closely the "classical" aesthetic espoused by Nietzsche.

And this is the quandary that makes both Nietzsche and Hofmannsthal exemplary practitioners of the philosophy of life: that society has little room for life's infusions, and community remains indifferent to living. Hofmannsthal-Chandos uses his exquisite prose to explain why he cannot—will not—return to his community, will not continue to exercise his calling as a writer, and Nietzsche, ever mindful and disparaging of the pitfalls of community, writes his *Zarathustra* "for all and none." Nietzsche tried through philosophy to convert souls to the living, while Hofmannsthal gave his best, as a poet, to inscribe himself in life (endearing himself to life). In both, language is challenged to its limits; in both, language ebbs at the point of crossing between life and community on the return from life.

If we agree that Nietzsche and Hofmannsthal were intrigued by the same medium—life—and if we agree also that this same medium both heightens and breaks the expressiveness of language, then it is safe to infer that contact with life is not without its danger. Hofmannsthal's Fortunio insisted that everything in life has a price and that everyone, strong or weak, gets his head bashed in eventually. For Chandos, the price of his alienating sojourns in the nondiscourse of life, where the values good and evil are meaningless, is his inability to return to the realm of his peers, where life goes on and continues to be governed by values. Chandos submerged himself in the medium of life, living dangerously for a time, but his eschewing of the common language remains, paradoxically, an act of life affirmation, since the document in which he expresses himself is a masterpiece in its own right—more than capable of expressing, even as he labors to express himself in the face of the inexpressible. Neither the life of Nietzsche's perception nor the life of Hofmannsthal's Chandos promises justice or any other special benefits for the human being; what each is able to make of it amounts to what each is able to inscribe.

The work of a writer—any writer—who tries to apprehend life by rendering it less abstract serves as the means by which his presence, singly, and his present, collectively, are suspended above chaos. Those who stand in abstract relation to life are themselves *abstracta*, as Nietzsche would say, and life perceived in the abstract may not seem chaotic, but it is. Hofmannsthal understood this and expressed it in the form of a parable, the epigram "Poets and Present." Because the poets are the shuddering ones, the ones who feel awe and trembling, they are the living; and because they are the living, it is given to them to be the holders and upholders of time, the vigilant ones upon whom the species rely, unknowingly, to establish presence out of chaos and keep a record.

The manner in which we assert ourselves in life, endear ourselves to life, and the visible record that distinguishes our lives and our present from the chaotic flux, is inscription. We inscribe ourselves upon the world; whatever weight, substance, and wit attaches to each of us, this must be inscribed as if the entire activity of a life were the act of inscribing on life. Inscribing ourselves is our fate, ultimately, but in the present, it is our work. "Inscription" ("Inschrift") is a poem of only four lines, and among the poems it possesses a rare, dramatic urgency:

> Do not deny the task that is upon you!
> Where awe grips you, there you have your calling:
> Not otherwise does life confess its meaning,
> And quickly chaos routs your fragile powers.
>
> (*KA*, I, 67)

On the surface these lines are an exhortation to embrace life in the present, to countenance one's work and to get it done. But like any inscription and any act of inscribing, the surface is penetrated and a lasting mark remains.

In the act of inscribing, a lasting record is created. I inscribe myself upon life by doing my work, by not shrinking from the task or waiting for life to reveal its designs to me. Inscribing myself into life, I am *cutting* myself into life, etching my spirit like an engraver. With and in time, I am asserting my presence so that the inscription will let me know where to find myself in an otherwise markerless chaos. Inscribing, I *feel* that I am here, and after chaos has had its way, my inscription remains.

The common people, Nietzsche claimed in *Zarathustra*, have no inkling of what spirit is (*Geist*). "Spirit is life that itself cuts into life; by its own torture it increases its own knowledge." [5] Well, if this is true of spirit per se, then let it also be true of all spirit, for all people, because spirit *is life*, and all life inscribes itself upon life, cuts into life at the expense of its own pain and presence. Are the furrows inscribed by the farmer into the earth any less vital than the philosopher's inscription of himself upon the page? And are the roads inscribed in the earth by laborers so that the farmer's goods can get to markets in the city—are these roads any less vital than the poet's inscription of himself upon the page? The crops themselves are blossoming inscriptions, bound for our tables, and the inscriptions we ingest become the inscriptions we choose or do not choose to leave behind.

5. Nietzsche, *Werke*, II, 361.

BIBLIOGRAPHY

Behler, Ernst. "Zur frühen sozialistischen Rezeption Nietzsches in Deutschland." *Nietzsche-Studien*, XIII (1984), 501–20.

Bennett, Benjamin. *Hugo von Hofmannsthal: The Theaters of Consciousness*. Cambridge, Eng., 1988.

Broch, Hermann. *Hofmannsthal und seine Zeit*. Frankfurt, 1974.

Cohn, Dorrit. "'Als Traum erzählt': The Case for a Freudian Reading of Hofmannsthal's 'Märchen der 672. Nacht.'" *Deutsche Vierteljahrsschrift für Literaturwissenschaft und Geistesgeschichte*, LIV (1980), 284–305.

Coleridge, Samuel Taylor. *The Complete Poetical Works of Samuel Taylor Coleridge*. Edited by E. H. Coleridge. 3rd ed. Oxford, 1962.

Del Caro, Adrian. "The Columbus Poems of Hölderlin and Nietzsche." *Colloquia Germanica*, XXI (1988), 144–58.

―――. "Hofmannsthal as a Paradigm of Nietzschean Influence on the Austrian fin de siècle." *Modern Austrian Literature*, XXII (1989), 81–95.

―――. *Hölderlin: The Poetics of Being*. Detroit, 1991.

―――. *Nietzsche contra Nietzsche: Creativity and the Anti-Romantic*. Baton Rouge, 1989.

―――. "The Pseudoman in Nietzsche, or The Threat of the Neuter." *New German Critique*, L (1990), 135–56.

―――. "Reception and Impact: The First Decade of Nietzsche in Germany." *Orbis Litterarum*, XXXVII (1982), 32–46.

Exner, Richard. *Hugo von Hofmannsthals "Lebenslied"*. Heidelberg, 1964.

Fischer, Jens Malte. *Fin de siècle*. Munich, 1978.

Goethe, Johann Wolfgang von. *Faust: Der Tragödie erster und zweiter Teil*. Edited by Erich Trunz. 10th ed. Munich, 1977.

―――. *Maximen und Reflexionen*. In *Johann Wolfgang von Goethe. Werke. Hamburger Ausgabe in 14 Bänden*, edited by Erich Trunz. 14 vols. Munich, 1982.

―――. *Wilhelm Meisters Lehrjahre*. In *Johann Wolfgang von Goethe. Werke. Hamburger Ausgabe in 14 Bänden*, edited by Erich Trunz. 14 vols. Munich, 1982.

Hamburger, Michael, ed. *Hugo von Hofmannsthal: Poems and Verse Plays*. New York, 1961.

Hanstein, Adalbert von. *Das jüngste Deutschland*. Leipzig, 1905.

Hardenberg, Friedrich von [Novalis]. *Die Lehrlinge zu Sais*. In *Novalis Schriften*, edited by Paul Kluckhohn and Richard Samuel. 4 vols. Stuttgart, 1960.

———. *Heinrich von Ofterdingen*. In *Novalis Schriften*, edited by Paul Kluckhohn and Richard Samuel. 4 vols. Stuttgart, 1960.

Heidegger, Martin. *Being and Time*. Translated by John Macquarrie and Edward Robinson. New York, 1962.

———. *Poetry, Language and Thought*. Translated by Albert Hofstadter. New York, 1971.

Heller, Erich. "Nietzsche and the Inarticulate." In *Nietzsche: Literature and Values*, edited by Volker Dürr, Reinhold Grimm, and Kathy Harms. Madison, 1988.

Hillebrand, Bruno. *Nietzsche und die deutsche Literatur*. Tübingen, 1978.

Hofmannsthal, Hugo von.

The following works are from *Hugo von Hofmannsthal: Sämtliche Werke. Kritische Ausgabe*. Veranstaltet vom Freien Deutschen Hochstift. 37 vols. Frankfurt, 1975–.

———. *Dramen 1*.

———. *Erzählungen 1*.

———. *Gedichte 1*.

———. *Gedichte 2*.

The following works are from *Hugo von Hofmannsthal: Gesammelte Werke in Einzelausgaben*, edited by Herbert Steiner. Fifteen volumes, inclusive of parts, nominally published in six volumes. Frankfurt, 1952–59.

———. "Das Gespräch über Gedichte." In *Prosa II*.

———. "Dichter und Leben." In *Prosa I*.

———. "Ein Brief [des Lord Chandos]." In *Prosa II*.

———. "Gabriele d'Annunzio. (I)." In *Prosa I*.

———. "Poesie und Leben." In *Prosa I*.

Hölderlin, Friedrich. *Gedichte Nach 1800*. Stuttgart, 1951. Vol. II, Pt. 1, of *Hölderlin: Sämtliche Werke*, edited by Friedrich Beissner. 8 vols.

Hoppe, Manfred. *Literatentum, Magie und Mystik im Frühwerk Hugo von Hofmannsthals*. Berlin, 1968.

Kaufmann, Walter, ed. and trans. *Basic Writings of Nietzsche*. New York, 1968.

Kiss, Endre. "Die Rezeption Friedrich Nietzsches in Ungarn bis 1918 / 19." *Nietzsche-Studien*, IX (1980), 268–84.

Kleist, Heinrich von. *Das Erdbeben in Chili*. In *Werke in einem Band*, edited by Helmut Sembdner. Munich, 1966.

Kolakowski, Leszek. *Bergson*. Oxford, 1985.

Lukács, Georg. *The Theory of the Novel*. Translated by Anna Bostock. Cambridge, Mass., 1971.

McGrath, William J. *Dionysian Art and Populist Politics in Austria*. New Haven, 1974.

Metzler, Werner. *Ursprung und Krise von Hofmannsthals Mystik*. Munich, 1956.

Meyer-Wendt, H. Jürgen. *Der frühe Hofmannsthal und die Gedankenwelt Nietzsches.* Heidelberg, 1973.

Mistry, Freny. "Hofmannsthal's 'Der Kaiser von China spricht.'" *Modern Language Review,* LXXI (1976), 66–72.

Mommsen, Katharina. "Loris und Nietzsche: Hofmannsthal's *Gestern* und Frühe Gedichte in Neuerer Sicht." *German Life and Letters,* XXXIV (1980), 49–63.

Nehring, Wolfgang. *Die Tat bei Hofmannsthal: Eine Untersuchung zu Hofmannsthals großen Dramen.* Stuttgart, 1966.

Nietzsche, Friedrich. *Friedrich Nietzsche: Werke in drei Bänden.* Edited by Karl Schlechta. 3 vols. Munich, 1966.

Poe, Edgar Allan. *Selected Prose, Poetry, and Eureka.* Edited by W. H. Auden. San Francisco, 1950.

Sartre, Jean-Paul. *"What is Literature?" and Other Essays.* Cambridge, Mass., 1988.

Schlegel, Friedrich. *Athenäums-Fragmente.* In *Kritische Friedrich-Schlegel-Ausgabe,* edited by Ernst Behler. 35 vols. Munich, 1958–.

———. *Dialogue on Poetry and Literary Aphorisms.* Edited and translated by Ernst Behler and Roman Struc. University Park, Pa., 1968.

Schopenhauer, Arthur. *Die Welt als Wille und Vorstellung.* In *Werke in zwei Bänden,* edited by Werner Brede. 2 vols. Munich, 1977.

Steffen, Hans. "Schopenhauer, Nietzsche, und die Dichtung Hofmannsthals." In *Nietzsche: Werk und Wirkungen,* edited by Hans Steffen. Göttingen, 1974.

Venturelli, Aldo. "Nietzsche in der Berggasse 19: Über die erste Nietzsche-Rezeption in Wien." *Nietzsche-Studien,* XIII (1984), 448–80.

Wackenroder, Wilhelm Heinrich. *Confessions and Fantasies.* Translated and annotated by Mary Hurst Schubert. University Park, Pa., 1971.

INDEX

Aesthetic (aestheticism): appearance sustains individual, 36; as a sub-sensual world, 114; classical, 5, 142; decadence, 5; falsifying nature, 34; justification of existence, 36; opposed by Hofmannsthal, 115; retreat into paralysis, 50; stylized life, 36; versus philosophy of life, 5, 44

All-connectedness, 58, 65, 69, 103, 110

Apollinian, 26

Awe: in *Faust*, 43–44; in shuddering of poet, 42–43, 143

Bergson, Henri: *durée*, 118; intuition, 119; profound self, 119; superficial self, 133

Bourget, Paul, 48

Brentano, Clemens, 80

Christianity: absolute morality of, 3; antilife values, 3; antiself, 6; as declining life, 11; emphasis on death, 7; eternal life, 136; fuels metaphysics, 10; Platonic-Christian bias, 10, 138

Coleridge, Samuel Taylor: "Phantom or Fact," 99–101

Community: discourse of, 141; Nietzsche's critique of, 13; poet mediates words, 49; poet's frame of reference, 16, 119, 142

Conviviality: awakening of speech, 116; contributes to transformation, 98, 126; dialogic powers, 99, 126; enables sharing, 98–99, 126

Danger: of apprehending time, 43; living dangerously, 43, 142; in relation to language, 6, 141

d'Annunzio, Gabriele: fictional characters, 50; influence on Hofmannsthal, 22

Darwin, Charles: struggle for existence, 11; survival of the fittest, 5

Dialogue: and conviviality, 99, 126; between earth and sky, 135; between friends, 69, 98; between man and world, 92–93, 117

Dionysus: amoral artistic phenomenon, 3, 72; awakens speech via tragedy, 116–17; as Bacchus with Muses, 116; bringer of divine fire, 99; equates wine with life, 67, 71; lyricist, 47; symbolizes abundant life, 67, 71, 117

Doubling (*Selbstverdoppelung*): as closed condition, 51; and detached observation, 48, 54; during transformation, 100, 136

Dream: approach to higher self, 62; conflated with knowledge, 24; as experience of double, 54; found, not dreamed, 59, 61, 98; inauthentic state, 94, 100; operates uninhibitedly, 65; portal to another world, 86; relation to preexistence, 54, 59, 65; as threshold to living, 62, 131; unity with man, 65; world of confusion, 86; wrested from life, 66–67

Education: lacks vitality, 17; as mere criticism, 20; in Nietzsche's age, 20; not internalized, 20

Eichendorff, Joseph von, 80, 127

Eternal recurrence: emphasis on life, 7; relation to the open, 115; Zarathustra's affirmation of, 8; Zarathustra's symbolic wedding to, 12

Fichte, Johann Gottlieb, 5

Fin die siècle: generation of, 24, 114; Hofmannsthal's relation to, 114–15; Nietzsche's influence on, 48, 138; not